THE
SPIRAL
NOTEBOOK

THE
SPIRAL
NOTEBOOK

THE AURORA THEATER SHOOTER
AND THE EPIDEMIC OF
MASS VIOLENCE COMMITTED
BY AMERICAN YOUTH

STEPHEN AND **JOYCE SINGULAR**

COUNTERPOINT | BERKELEY, CALIFORNIA

Library of Congress Cataloging-in-Publication Data is available
ISBN 978-1-61902-534-9

Cover design by Michael Kellner
Interior design by Elyse Strongin, Neuwirth & Associates, Inc.

COUNTERPOINT
2560 Ninth Street, Suite 318
Berkeley, CA 94710
www.counterpointpress.com

Printed in the United States of America
Distributed by Publishers Group West

10 9 8 7 6 5 4 3 2 1

To Eric

AUTHORS' NOTE

On the morning of July 20, 2012, we drove to the Aurora apartment of James Holmes and then to the Century 16 movie complex. Several hours earlier at this theater, Holmes had unleashed the largest mass shooting in U.S. history, and news reports of the event were still breaking across the country and around the world. Since his living space and the crime scene were only a few miles from our Denver home, we wanted to see the locations for ourselves—marking the beginning of an investigative journey that would last for the next two and a half years.

The first people we interviewed were Holmes's neighbors, who were standing a few hundred yards from his blocked-off apartment building, now wired with explosives and ready to blow. As the bomb squad worked to defuse the situation, the locals stared at the building in bewilderment and talked about what had happened in the theater. We continued on to Century 16, and in an adjacent parking lot we spoke to moviegoers who'd survived the massacre. Police had just released the witnesses from their custody.

Over the next thirty months, we attended all of the significant legal proceedings for Holmes. These included motion hearings, evidentiary hearings, hearings on the spiral notebook itself, and those on psychiatric issues, the death penalty, and the debate over criminal sanity versus insanity. Most importantly, in January 2013 we sat through the preliminary hearing, where the prosecution outlined its case against Holmes. We heard two full days of police testimony, which helped us to reconstruct a timeline of Holmes's movements leading up to, during, and following the massacre. This process was aided by our own investigations and by numerous journalistic sources, both local and national, devoted to uncovering and tracking Holmes's behavior. In addition to this, we conducted personal interviews with many people and businesses in and around the Anschutz CU campus, most speaking to us under the condition of anonymity. We were able to talk with several staff members in the graduate department of CU, again under the condition of anonymity. None spoke directly about the case itself, but only about Holmes's routine at the school, offering a sense of who he was before he became infamous.

We visited Anschutz and retraced Holmes's steps around the campus. We saw his classrooms, his lab, and where he'd had his therapy sessions in the spring of 2012. In 2013 and 2014, we sat in on the kinds of lectures on the brain and mental illness that Holmes might have attended had he not been incarcerated. We went to the tavern where he drank in the evenings and to the places in his neighborhood where he shopped or ate his meals. Many years before the massacre, we'd watched films at the theater where the shootings occurred, and we returned to the movie complex after it had been remodeled and renamed following the tragedy. All of these things provided us with a more intimate feeling for the young man's life as he made his descent into violence during his year in Aurora.

Starting in the summer of 2012 we also began a series of interviews that lasted over two years and included psychologists, psychiatrists, first responders, psycho-pharmacologists, private investigators, teachers, and many, many young people throughout the nation. Because the thousands of pages of legal documents the shootings had generated were sealed and all of the principals in the case were under a gag order, we couldn't approach this as a true crime story and put together a conventional narrative of Holmes's actions, as we'd done in many previous books. Instead of writing about one mass shooter, we started to explore the society and the generation that had produced not just Holmes, but so many other young male killers. This turned out to be our deeper interest, partially because we had a son not much younger than Holmes himself. By taking our investigation outside of the courtroom, we stumbled onto a much larger stage.

During those thirty months of investigation, we talked to anyone who'd speak with us about the mass-shooting phenomenon: from teenagers to those in their eighties and nineties; from people we met at social gatherings to those we ran into at coffee shops. Everyone in America is a part of this story, and most everyone, if probed a little, has something to say about it. Our job, first and foremost, was to start the conversation. Because of the impact and reach of social media, most young people were much more comfortable and much more open when speaking with us if their names weren't used. All of these voices, whether they're in the book or not, make up the fabric of this story. They offer a portrait of America passing through a scourge of violence new to our national experience.

It's both reflexive and normal to recoil from the phenomenon of mass shootings. But that reflex hasn't solved the problem or made it vanish. In the summer of 2012, we decided to move toward this phenomenon rather than away from it to see if we could learn something new about ourselves, our own family, and our society.

THE
SPIRAL
NOTEBOOK

PROLOGUE

"You Don't Understand How I Grew Up"

Our son's formative years in Denver were bookended by two mass tragedies. The first was at Columbine High on April 20, 1999, when a pair of teenagers walked into the school and opened fire, killing twelve students, a teacher, and themselves. This happened about fifteen miles from our home when Eric was five and too young to understand the significance of the event. But he was not too young to pick up on the feeling in the city or our house that day—one of profound sadness. Words seemed inadequate to the occasion; nobody knew what to say and it was uncomfortable to make eye contact on the street. The violence was close enough to send a message to everyone: Something is fundamentally wrong and this is the end result of it. Don't take anything for granted, including your next breath.

The second bookend was the Aurora Theater shooting, seven miles from our home, unleashed just after midnight on July 12, 2012. Eric was almost nineteen and a sophomore at the University of Colorado, studying sociology. The morning following this massacre, which left twelve dead and seventy others wounded, we decided to drive out to the crime scenes. We had, after all, spent the past two decades working as investigative journalists and writing books about American violence. Our interest was in understanding more about the psychology of those who committed murder, but we'd always covered these events from a distance—as reporters conducting interviews or as observers sitting in courtrooms. That distance was now gone. The carnage in Aurora was even closer to us than it had been at Columbine. Our family had watched many films together in Theater Nine of the Aurora movie complex, where the shootings had taken place.

The war, as people had said in the 1960s when protesting the fighting in Vietnam, had come home.

On the morning of July 20, we first visited the bomb-rigged apartment of the Aurora shooter and watched demolition experts use cherry pickers to try to defuse the explosives he'd built in his living space before going to the theater. Standing behind the yellow police tape, we talked with his stunned neighbors. Scores of them were out on the street, trying to make sense of what they were seeing and wearing the same numb expression we'd seen thirteen year earlier, after Columbine.

We then drove on to the parking lot behind the theater itself, where journalists and media personnel were already pouring into suburban Denver from across the nation. By now, their movements and attitudes had become routine when covering America's latest mass shooting. They looked both urgent and nonchalant. Last night another young man, who did not come from impoverished circumstances, had done something unimaginable, although we'd seen these same actions again and again and again. Each time, the violence seemed more unbelievable, and each time the shock and horror were fresh and overwhelming. In the parking lot, we stood in the scorching sunlight and talked with a couple of survivors of the shooting. They'd just been interviewed by the police and then released after a very long night. They looked traumatized yet unable to go home.

We drove back to the house, where Eric was scouring websites for information about the event. During his high school years, like many teenagers, he hadn't shared much with us. If he wasn't exactly secretive, he definitely kept to himself, and we never knew exactly what he was thinking.

By July 2012, he'd finished his first year of college and was slowly opening up, speaking about his classes and which professors had influenced him the most. When we asked him what he thought about the Aurora shooting, he seemed reluctant to tell us, as if we might not like his answer.

We probed a little more until he said, "You don't understand how I grew up."

"What do you mean?" Joyce said.

"You just don't get it," he told her. "No offense, but you're too old."

"Get what?"

"How everyone my age grew up and what we've experienced."

"What have you experienced?"

"A lot of stuff you didn't when you were young. People your age don't know anything about this or why these shootings keep happening."

His tone was serious and one we'd never quite heard before, as if he were telling us something very important to him, but something he thought we might dismiss.

We traded confused looks, taken aback. Like most people, we thought of ourselves as decent enough parents. We'd raised our only child in a good neighborhood, sent him to good schools, monitored his education, and helped with homework, trying to do all the things mothers and fathers who care about their children do. We didn't see our parenting as unusual, except in one regard. Both of us had worked at home virtually the entire time he'd been a youngster and adolescent. That had given us even more time to observe him and try to set him on a good path.

So what had we missed? What were we too old to "get"?

We came from the antiwar generation of the 1960s and had embraced "peace, love, and understanding" at the level of something more than a media cliché. We'd actually believed in those things and had tried to hold onto some of that belief as we'd aged. What had happened in America between our youth and his? What was behind the mass-shooting phenomenon?

In case after case, we'd watched young men open fire with assault-style, military weapons, as if they were at war with our society. More often than not, they choose to die in the resulting gunfire with the police. Since the 1990s, this had occurred far too many times to be seen as a set of random occurrences. The unthinkable had become not just thinkable, but virtually commonplace. The killers often attacked at schools or institutions of higher learning, and on college campuses now administrators and students regularly held drills, complete with fake blood and faux bullets, for what to do when an "active shooter" was on the premises or in the classroom. In our youth, we'd had to crawl under our desks at school in case the Soviets launched a missile attack on the United States, but even then, that seemed a distant possibility. It never happened. Mass shootings happened all the time.

It was beyond disturbing that young men around our son's age had been engaging in this kind of violence against the American population. What had gone wrong? What was Eric trying to tell us about his generation and the latest round of shootings in Aurora?

The most obvious reason we wanted to know more about this was because no one was out of the line of fire. The chances of being targeted by a serial killer were very slim, but the possibility of sending your child to school one morning and never seeing him or her again had become a real threat. The idea of attending a benign entertainment event, like a movie, and getting gunned down was no longer unimaginable. Mass violence in America had become all but predictable.

Because we were raising a son in the age of such violence, we were determined to learn more.

■ ■ ■

In the coming weeks, Eric would make this same remark about his growing up a few more times before it began to sink in. He seemed to have little trouble grasping why males around his age were doing such horrific things.

He also said, "I know kids who could do what James Holmes did. I understand some of their feelings."

These comments were the starting point for this book, and they led to many other discussions with our son as we began to explore what he meant. This process took time, but as our dialogue with him deepened, so did our journey toward putting together this story. All of this was a departure from the work we'd been involved in for the past twenty years. We were approaching the subject not just as investigative journalists, but as parents and members of a family and a community.

Since the early 1990s, we'd written numerous books about many high-profile criminal cases, where violence intersected with larger social issues, like racism or religious terrorism or the dangers of the Internet. We'd researched legal documents, conducted hundreds or thousands of interviews, and spent countless hours in courtrooms looking at evidence and listening to witness testimony. From the beginning, nothing in the James Holmes case would conform to this pattern. He wasn't a serial murderer, a predator, a power-crazed religious leader, or a political assassin. Like many of the other young mass shooters, he seemed intent on making a statement about the society he was living in, but what kind of statement? Grappling with that question would be difficult enough, but three days after the Aurora shootings, everyone connected to the massacre was placed under a gag order that would last for the duration of the case. The attorneys, police, psychiatrists, and other witnesses couldn't talk to anyone about anything (though this didn't prevent us from speaking with other mental health experts or from seeking out any information we could find from secondary sources).

More than two and a half years went by with the gag order in place, but we attended nearly every Holmes legal proceeding and were in the courtroom during the preliminary hearing for the defendant in January 2013, when prosecutors had to lay out their basic case against him. This provided copious police testimony and numerous details about Holmes's preparation for the crime. Still, many conventional areas of inquiry, especially regarding his background and medical records, were off-limits.

Where did that leave us?

With turning to people of Holmes's generation, beginning with our son and expanding outward from there. We've been called "forensic journalists," but we weren't looking at this story in terms of physical evidence. Everyone knew the details of what had happened in Aurora and that Holmes had committed mass murder. We were trying to identify the cultural and emotional forces driving the young shooters.

Something has changed in the underlying atmosphere of America between the 1960s and the new millennium, something that we wanted to understand more about.

The Spiral Notebook was written to explore these questions and issues. Our intention is to open up and add to a dialogue around this difficult subject. Our intention is not to deliver a criticism of any other approach to penetrating the recent rash of mass violence. Psychiatric models, when it comes to mass shootings, tend to focus on the perpetrators as aberrant individuals. We've attempted something else—looking at the aberrations of an entire society. From the beginning, our son's message to us was quite clear: people our age (over fifty) don't really understand the influences affecting him and his friends, and how those influences are as pervasive and important as anything else in their lives. If one didn't have something to counteract these factors—good relationships, a solid and honest connection with one's parents, self-esteem, and self-control—one could easily slide into serious problems, or even violence.

We've written *The Spiral Notebook* in the hope that parents, educators, politicians, those in the media, and citizens young and old will gain something from our explorations. In our line of work, we're constantly asked, "Why do you want to write about *that*? Why focus on such dark topics? Why do you want to spend your time delving into ugly things when there are so many lighter and more positive stories?"

We could respond with a few questions of our own. Has ignoring the mass shooting "epidemic," as many have called it, made it go away? Or has it only gotten worse? What if this phenomenon isn't just the product of a handful of deranged minds, but the natural outcome of what our society has recently supported and encouraged? What if we could see ourselves as participants in these events and not merely as victims of them? What if our awareness of this process is just beginning? And what if we actually had the power to do something to enact change?

In the summer of 2012, we didn't want to hear everything our son had to tell us about his growing up, but we listened. It wasn't that we'd consciously avoided this subject with him; we just didn't know where to begin. Taking the lead from Eric, we sought out the thoughts and feelings of other people in their twenties and have given them a platform for expression in this book. We've chosen to weave their information in and around the story of James Holmes, who committed one of the largest mass shootings in U.S. history. We did this because the more we looked into his case, the more it opened up into much larger subjects: legal and illegal drugs and the young; violent fantasy entertainment and the young; our national experience since 9/11 and the young; mental illness and the young; a sense of hopelessness and the young; and spirituality (or the lack of it) and the young. Unlike many of the shooters, Holmes survived his massacre and has since gone through an extensive legal and mental health evaluation process. This too has become a very revealing part of his story.

In addition to these things, Holmes was an exceptionally bright young man, the model of a budding American scientist on the way to success. He had everything to work for and to live for. What caused his transformation from a highly motivated and productive student into someone committed to mass destruction? What pushed him into a fantasy realm of violence that became all too real?

The most unsettling part of this book is that an individual, like a nation, can gradually slip into a state of madness with hardly anyone noticing. A person working inside an environment of very intelligent, well-educated, and seemingly observant people can evolve into a killing machine—with nobody paying attention or doing anything to stop him. For months, no one saw the changes in James Holmes or picked up on the signs for what he was turning into and planning. Or if someone did, he or she chose not to speak up. Better to look away and not say anything that might cause a disruption. Better to keep still and pretend that everything would turn out fine.

■ ■ ■

As the twentysomething generation spoke to us, two themes repeatedly emerged. The first echoed our son's point of view: older Americans didn't know or understand much about their experience. They'd come of age when the future seemed quite limited, if not choked off. Climate change, economic collapse, Y2K, global terrorism, the end of the world in December 2012—there's always another apocalypse just around the corner. If there weren't enough real threats, the movie industry kept churning out one terrifying or dystopian vision of tomorrow after another. They were filled with superheroes who wielded power by killing as many others as they could.

The second theme was that this generation was ready—more than ready—for fundamental change, structural social and political change, in many different ways. No matter what else they brought up, this was the constant drumbeat: something new needs to come, a new way of interacting and cooperating both within our institutions and at the personal level. Cultural wars and public demonizing are nothing but broken tools. Political division and hatred have led only to more division and hatred. Bullying, whether by the government or the media or the kid next door, is toxic and creates consequences that we're only beginning to glimpse. Being "right" and making someone else "wrong" is a useless strategy if it only leads to gridlock. When do we actually start to confront and solve problems, instead of engaging in the anger, fear, and finger-pointing that's characterized American life over the past few decades?

In selecting which young people to quote in these pages, we naturally had to make choices. Our only requirement was that they had something of relevance to say on the issues noted above. After decades of journalistic experience, we've learned a simple truth. Some interview subjects have more to offer than others. In this case, they were willing to say even more if their names were not being used, in large part because of the pressures and reach of social media, so we've kept them anonymous.

If their voices occasionally convey despair, underneath that despair runs a deep sense of idealism and the age-old American desire to make the future better. Their voices provide the best core of hope in the story you are about to read. It isn't being offered as a sociological study or a clinical analysis of crime, but as a modest and intimate look at one family's exploration of a new form of American terrorism.

SUPERHERO

From a twenty-seven-year-old female:

> *James Holmes is that thing in the air that everyone kind of senses is there and is wrong with our society, but no one can actually see it or put a finger on it. It's that thing we feel all around us now. We know it's there and we know we should do something about it, but we seem paralyzed to stand up and do anything.*

I

The dark figure had parked the white Hyundai hatchback behind
Theater Nine and was casually leaning on the open door on the driv-
er's side. He was sweating heavily inside his SWAT gear: a bulky black
coat, slick black pants made of windbreaker material, a gas mask, a
ballistic helmet, an urban assault vest, shin guards, a throat guard, and
a groin protector. An empty sling lay across the chest, made to hold
a rifle. Beneath the outerwear was another layer of dark, bullet-proof
leggings, like those worn by a cop on a dangerous mission or a soldier
headed into combat. The person wrapped inside the gear was dressed
for warfare, like an American superhero of the kind found in action
films and comic books.

With police lights spinning and sirens whining, Patrolman Jason
Obiatt pulled in next to the white vehicle, studying the calm shape
beside the Hyundai. It had to be another officer, Obiatt decided, one
who'd received the same 911 call he did and arrived at the theater
moments before him. At 12:38 a.m., a series of 911 bulletins had
spread out across Aurora and greater Denver about a shooting at the
Century 16 movie complex. From every direction, patrol cars and
ambulances were racing to this location.

Obiatt looked more closely at the figure, surprised at the pos-
ture and how the person inside the SWAT outfit showed no sense
of urgency at this massive crime scene. His movements—if it was a

he—weren't rushed or anxious. He seemed completely at ease, and on closer inspection his uniform wasn't exactly standard issue; the gas mask was different.

Stepping out of his patrol car and approaching the Hyundai, Obiatt kept his eyes on the figure's hands resting atop the vehicle. Near them was a pistol, probably a semiautomatic, 40-round Glock.

Drawing his own firearm, Obiatt was only seven or eight steps away and advanced cautiously.

"Get your hands down on the ground!" he ordered, looking in the car for others, seeing no one else.

The figure remained still.

"Get down on the ground!"

The figure complied, but in the same unhurried manner, lowering himself to the pavement. As he lay facing the asphalt, a handgun magazine fell from his pocket. Then another tumbled out.

The officer grabbed him and dragged him ten feet over to a Dumpster. He cuffed his wrists, frisked him for weapons.

The figure was perfectly compliant.

Obiatt couldn't feel any weapons, but the individual had on so much body armor that he thought he might be missing something tucked around the waist or hidden in a pant leg. He kept searching and fumbling within all the protective gear, finding a knife inside a belt and one more in a secret compartment.

"Get up!" he said. "You're under arrest."

The figure stood up.

Obiatt saw another officer, Aaron Blue, coming across the parking lot to assist him.

The men conferred, and Blue pulled out a police knife and began to cut items of clothing from the suspect's body. They smelled acrid, like tear gas. Blue snipped off as many layers as he could, but the material was difficult to slice through and still concealed several items, including an iPod Touch. The officer put away the knife and proceeded to undress the thin, pale young man, right down to his ripped white

T-shirt, underwear, and socks. He emitted a harsh odor, but he didn't appear or smell drunk.

Obiatt rejoined Blue and observed the skinny figure. In his six years on the Aurora police force, Obiatt had made numerous arrests under all kinds of conditions. He knew that whenever you confronted or tried to move a suspect, you should anticipate resistance. When people resisted, you could feel muscular tension rippling through their bodies, but not this time. Obiatt had never seen anyone in this situation so relaxed or with so little verbal or emotional response. He seemed detached in every way.

His arms, shoulders, and torso had gone slack, as if all of his energy and adrenalin had been spent and he was now at peace. The mission was over, the goal achieved. He could finally sit back and look at what he'd created, like a painter admiring his completed canvas or a film director watching the daily rushes of his latest picture or a soldier after conquering the enemy.

Virtually undressed, he was lean and wiry, probably in his mid-twenties, although the officers hadn't yet seen his face. They now removed his gas mask, revealing a shock of bright orange hair.

"I'm The Joker," he mumbled.

The men exchanged glances, startled by the hair, by this remark, and by his huge pupils.

They asked if he had any other firearms besides the Glock.

"Yes," he replied evenly. "Four of them."

Officer Blue reached inside the suspect's pants pockets, locating a wallet and counting $280 in cash. He pulled out a University of Colorado ID card, a credit card, a health insurance card, and a driver's license. The latter belonged to James Holmes of 1690 Paris Street, in Aurora, four miles north of the theater.

Officer Blue came closer. "Are there any explosives?"

"Yes."

"Where are they?"

"In my apartment."

"Are they ready to go off?"

"Yes. If you trip the wires."

"What are they?"

"IEDs."

Improvised Explosive Devices, also known as "roadside bombs," could be detonated by remote control. In recent years, they'd been widely employed as unconventional military weapons in terrorist actions against the United States. By the end of 2007, they were responsible for nearly two-thirds of the Coalition deaths in the war with Iraq. They'd caused roughly the same number of casualties in the ongoing fighting in Afghanistan, including 3,200 casualties in 2011 alone. IEDs were most effective at maiming or removing people's limbs.

Blue walked away from the two men, passing along the name, address, and information about the explosives to his fellow officers. As he did so, more and more police vehicles, fire engines, and emergency medical personnel were arriving at the theater, its parking lot illuminated by splashes of red and yellow lights and echoing with sirens and horns. Because of all the patrol cars now on the scene, ambulances couldn't get near the complex and had been directed to a staging area to await instructions. Fire trucks had jumped over cement curbs and medians, while black-and-white police cars had driven up a steep grassy slope. In the middle of this vast traffic jam, nearly a thousand moviegoers were fleeing from all the doors of Century 16, some bleeding, running toward the police, and screaming.

At 12:38, Kevin Quinonez made the initial 911 call from inside the theater, and by 12:41 police cars had begun arriving at the complex. At 12:45, forty more such calls had gone out, and paramedics from Engine 8 were already triaging patients at the northwest corner of Century 16.

At 12:46, a police officer called into dispatch and said, "Rescue inside the auditorium. Multiple victims."

At 12:47, another report said, "Seven down in Theater Nine."

A bomb squad had reached Holmes's vehicle. They broke the Hyundai's dark-tinted windows and looked inside, seeing a throat protector, a cell phone, and a hard plastic gun case. They deployed a two-foot-tall robot to go into the car and search for other weapons or explosives. Two hundred and twenty-three police officers from Denver and Aurora were descending on the complex.

II

When Officer Justin Grizzle approached Holmes to ask again if he was alone at the complex, the young man answered not in words, but with a self-satisfied smirk that Grizzle found maddening. He saw a green dot, like a laser beam, aimed at him from some bushes next to the parking lot. A second shooter must have been in there, training his weapon on the police, or it could have been a detonating mechanism. The dot disappeared and Grizzle realized that it had come from the Glock lying on the roof of the Hyundai.

On the pavement at the rear emergency exit door leading into Theater Nine, Grizzle saw an AR-15 semiautomatic rifle with a magazine still in it. As he moved toward the firearm, streams of moviegoers charged out of the exit, yelling, "Help me! Help me! Help me!"

Reaching for his handgun and steeling himself, Grizzle walked into Theater Nine, slipping on pools of blood. Tear gas burned his eyes and throat. He was crying now and his nose had begun to run. Strobe lights whirled above him, alarm bells clanged, and ringing cell phones filled the air. Behind him, a blaring movie—the most recent Batman film, *The Dark Knight Rises*, which was having its midnight premiere at many locations across the country—played on a huge screen. The picture had just started and the dialogue boomed out across the theater. The light and the noise and the enlarged characters standing over his shoulder all added to Grizzle's sense of disorientation. Sounds and colors and smoke and shrieks collided with so much tear gas he could barely breathe.

Through the fog, he saw bodies lying motionless and other bodies cowering in the first several rows of seats; other bodies crawled up the aisles on hands and knees and still others raced for the exits. When they reached the lobby, they were hustled by theater employees outside or told to crouch down behind the concession stands. Officers bent over some of the corpses and checked them for booby traps.

Blood, popcorn, and 249 live rounds of ammunition mingled together on the floor of Theater Nine. As Grizzle moved toward the wounded, other policemen began appearing inside the smoke, booming out instructions, opening doors to let out the tear gas, and ripping down the movie screen to see if anyone was hiding behind it. No one was.

"Get 'em out of here!" they commanded back and forth, improvising a triage section for those closest to death.

If the victims could talk, they were carted away from the exits to await help from emergency medical personnel. If they couldn't talk, they were kept by the theater doors and offered help now.

Grizzle grabbed two of the wounded and steered them outside toward his patrol car; waiting for the stalled ambulances was no longer an option. As he settled the pair into the vehicle's seats, he thought: *I don't want anyone else to die. No one else can die . . .*

With his siren whirring, he wended his way out of the parking lot and took off for the Aurora South Medical Center. He was violating protocol because patrol cars weren't supposed to transport the wounded to hospitals, but he felt he had no choice.

In the rear seat was Ashley Moser, pregnant and bleeding heavily from gunshot wounds to the head and chest. Sitting next to Grizzle was her husband, Ian Sullivan.

"That's my wife in the back," Ian said over and over again. "That's my wife. Is she going to live?"

Grizzle kept driving.

"Where's my six-year-old daughter?" the man asked.

Grizzle didn't know where Veronica Moser-Sullivan was, so he didn't answer.

"You have to turn around and go find her!" Ian said.

The officer kept driving as fast as he thought he safely could.

"You have to go back and get her!"

Grizzle drove on.

Ian flung open the passenger door to jump out of the speeding patrol car, but the officer caught him by the arm and yanked him back inside.

"*Don't!*" Grizzle screamed.

Ian didn't try it again.

After dropping off the two victims at the hospital, Grizzle went back to the theater to pick up others, repeating this pattern twice more before the night was over. Only later, after all the trips were finished and the night was giving way to dawn, did he learn that six-year-old Veronica Moser-Sullivan had been hit four times and was dead.

On his third trip in the early morning hours of July 20, Grizzle drove a badly wounded man named Caleb Medley to the University of Colorado Hospital, one of twenty-three victims taken to this facility—where Holmes had been in graduate school a few weeks earlier—since other emergency rooms in the area were filled up.

In the back seat, Medley's breathing made what Grizzle described as a "God-awful sound," but that sound was much better than when he stopped breathing altogether.

Each time it ceased, Grizzle yelled over his shoulder, "Don't you fucking die on me! Don't you fucking die!"

Every time he said this, Caleb started breathing again, slowly but steadily keeping the air moving through his lungs.

At the hospital, the doctors saved Caleb's life, but more than a year later he'd still be using a wheelchair.

According to a report on the emergency response to the Aurora shootings delivered more than two years later, by breaking protocol and transporting the wounded in patrol cars instead of ambulances, Grizzle and other officers saved all of the lives that night that could have been saved.

From a twenty-one-year-old male college student in Missouri:

Sometimes, I just want to blow. The only thing that stops me is my own sense of self-control. Take that away and I just don't know what would happen. I don't think any of us feel a part of a real community anymore or feel that we know one another. Being disconnected socially is the start of the problem.

III

The police lowered Holmes into the back of a patrol car, strapped him in, and drove him to the Aurora City Detention Center. By 2:44 a.m., APD Detectives Chuck Mehl and Craig Appel were beginning their initial interview with the suspect. They asked if he needed anything, like water or oxygen, but he declined. His skin was raw from being dragged to a Dumpster behind the theater, but the damage wasn't serious enough to warrant medical treatment.

The detectives had wrapped paper bags over his hands to preserve gunpowder residue or other evidence, a standard procedure in crimes involving firearms. As the men gathered at a table, Holmes raised his hands and waved the paper bags around in the air as if they were finger puppets. The veteran officers had never seen this before. Holmes lowered the bags and ripped a staple out of the table, trying to ram it into an electrical socket.

They stopped him, stunned by his bizarre behavior.

"Do you need help?" one asked.

"Like in counseling?"

"No. Like in paramedics. We want to make this easy for you."

"No."

He nodded at some nearby evidence bags and wondered aloud if they were used to hold popcorn.

The men shook their heads. They hadn't yet given Holmes his

Miranda warning, that he had the right to remain silent and the right to consult with an attorney and to have an attorney present during questioning. If he were indigent, a lawyer would be provided to represent him at no cost.

Seven minutes into the interview, Holmes said, "I want to invoke my Sixth Amendment rights."

"So you're invoking your right to counsel?" Mehl asked.

"Yes. I want an attorney."

The officers prodded a little more before the discussion came to an end.

A number of things about the twenty-four-year-old suspect were unusual—starting with his appearance, his demeanor, and his apparent intelligence (many people being interrogated were not aware of their Sixth Amendment rights). Some other things about him were no longer that odd. In the past two decades, mass shootings had become almost predictable across America. In about 60 percent of these cases, the killer or killers decided to die during the massacre. They either committed suicide, as Eric Harris and Dylan Klebold had done inside Columbine High School in suburban Denver in April 1999, or committed "suicide by cop," offering violent resistance to the arresting officers, who shot them to death.

Holmes had done neither. He'd surrendered peacefully and had been fully accommodating with those who'd put him in a patrol car and taken him to the station. He'd been cooperative right up until asking for a lawyer. Like The Joker in *The Dark Knight*, he'd decided to live and to watch what he'd set in motion. As a result, he was going to go through an astonishingly lengthy legal process that was now only a few hours old. This process would confound countless observers of the case and force lawyers and judges to face issues with the potential of making U.S. judicial history—most notably, issues concerning doctor-patient confidentiality and criminal insanity. By staying alive, Holmes was going to put America on trial for how to deal with this new epidemic of mass violence.

With just one of his guns, the AR-15, he'd fired thirty rounds in twenty-seven seconds. In something less than two minutes, he'd shot bullets or bullet fragments into 238 theater seats and left twelve people dead, with ten of the bodies still inside Century 16. Seventy other moviegoers had been wounded (fifteen of them permanently), and all were on their way to hospitals or already checked in. Among the fatalities were Jessica Ghawi, twenty-four, an aspiring sportscaster; Jesse Childress, twenty-nine, a member of an Air Force skydiving team; and Gordon Cowden, fifty-one, who'd taken his two teenage daughters to the theater.

Within the next few days, Ashley Moser would have a miscarriage. Because she was paralyzed from her injuries, her six-year-old daughter's funeral would be delayed for three months until Ashley was able to attend the service.

■ ■ ■

On average, 196 people are shot in America every day, yet nobody seems to know where all the violence is coming from. Tonight it had come to Aurora, a city of 335,000 just east of Denver, but it would soon explode again at a Sikh temple in Wisconsin; at a college in Texas; at several other venues; and then finally, near the end of the year, at Sandy Hook Elementary in Newtown, Connecticut. The last massacre of 2012 left twenty children and eight adults dead, including the shooter himself, twenty-year-old Adam Lanza, who'd lived with his mother in a home stockpiled with weapons.

Around Newtown, Lanza had been known as noticeably strange and far more likely to do something horrific than, say, James Holmes. In the four months between the Aurora shootings and those at Sandy Hook, Lanza had studied Holmes and seemingly snapped because his mother was planning to commit him to a psychiatric facility.

Following Newtown, the questions around mass shootings had at last become too large to ignore or dismiss. For a few weeks, the nation's airwaves were filled with dialogue about this subject. Had we finally reached a tipping point that left us ready to attempt to do *something* to end the carnage? What was the driving force behind all this bloodshed, and how might it be lessened, if not stopped? Why did America have far more of these events than any other developed nation in the world?

For the crimes of burglary, assault, robbery, and theft, the United States had similar numbers to other developed countries. But our country's gun homicide rate was about eleven thousand a year—thirty times higher, for example, than France's or Australia's, according to the U.N. Office on Drugs and Crime. It was twelve times higher than in most other comparable nations. In the first *five months* following the Newtown massacre, after the dialogue had begun to fade and people turned to other matters, the number of American gun deaths would exceed the total number of U.S. troops killed in the eight-year Iraq war: 4,499 to 4,409, based on statistics released by the Department of Defense.

Of the 196 people shot in the nation on an average day, eighty-six died. According to the Centers for Disease Control and Prevention, nearly one child or teen *per hour* was now injured by a firearm—hurt seriously enough to require hospitalization. For those fifteen to nineteen, firearm injuries remained the second leading cause of death, behind only car wrecks.

Mass killers were now targeting Americans almost once every two weeks. Based on FBI records from 2006–2010, 156 of these homicidal rampages had met the Feds' definition of mass shootings, where four or more people had died. Earlier decades in America were much worse in terms of overall rates of violent crime, but saw far fewer mass shootings. In the 1980s, the country had experienced eighteen of them. By the 1990s, there were fifty-four such events, and the 2000s had seen eighty-seven.

In the dozen years after September 11, 2001, our nation saw less than twenty terror-related deaths on American soil—but nearly

364,000 deaths caused by privately owned firearms. It cost the nation more than $2 billion a year in hospital charges to treat victims of gun-related wounds, and the average cost per victim was $75,884. An Urban Institute study reported that more than 80 percent of gun violence was paid for by taxpayers through Medicaid or other publicly funded programs.

Newtown had been anything but a tipping point in slowing down this phenomenon. In the fourteen months following that massacre, America would see a school shooting an average of every ten days—or eighty-eight more over the next two years. Instead of turning around the trend, Sandy Hook had made it worse.

From a twenty-four-year-old female graduate student:

> These mass shootings are there to wake us up to our own worst behavior and our own involvement in the violence. They're to make us think and to take action. It's up to us to figure all this out and to try to stop it—because by the time these people commit these murders, their lives are over and they've already checked out.

IV

As the detectives tried unsuccessfully to interrogate Holmes, a bomb squad rushed to his three-story Aurora apartment complex at 1690 Paris Street. When they arrived, they were confronted with something so disturbing that the best option seemed to be blowing up the entire structure.

"We knew that building would go," Aurora police Lt. Thomas Wilkes, the incident commander at the scene, said later. "The idea was, 'Can we defend the other buildings around it?'"

It was too dangerous to send human beings in to investigate what Holmes had devised inside his third-floor, 800-square-foot living space. The bomb experts didn't know how many IEDs were placed within these walls, what kinds of explosives they contained, and how far the damage could reach if detonated. Would other nearby buildings come down? Would hazardous fumes endanger people blocks away? The first step was evacuating the entire building, which a SWAT team did in the middle of the night.

Several officers maneuvered a 480-pound robot into the building and up the stairs to Holmes's apartment. While the robot blasted open the front door, the bomb squad sat outside in a van and watched through a camera attached to the robot. Inside Holmes's living space, they detected a booby-trapped explosive that had just cleared the swinging front door, three clusters of incendiary devices, black balls resembling fireworks, a half-opened soda bottle, and flashing LED lights. A trip wire led across the room to an open thermos of clear liquid, and in the kitchen, a frying pan, precariously perched on the stove, held a dark-colored substance. Mortar shells and white powder were scattered on the floor. Other wires, like triggering devices, streamed off the LED lights. The squad also saw something that looked like napalm.

A strong gas smell poured from the apartment, so they decided not to send the robot in any farther. One spark could ignite everything. They examined more images from the camera and spotted an antenna, indicating that the explosives were likely attached to a remote device, but where was it?

■ ■ ■

By the time the police had escorted Holmes to his cell at three a.m., other inmates had already heard about the massacre. They spewed taunts at the young man—calling him a "kid killer" because of reports that he'd shot children at the theater—and promised revenge if they got him alone in the jail. Realizing that he was in danger, officials at the detention center placed Holmes in a bulletproof vest, his hands cuffed behind him and his legs shackled. None of this kept him from flailing wildly, screaming at corrections officers, lurching and spitting so aggressively that he had to be restrained.

"Let's just say he hasn't shown any remorse," a jail employee later told the *New York Daily News* about the suspect's first few hours of incarceration. "He thinks he's acting in a movie."

Denver's alternative paper *Westword* would eventually report on Holmes's first night in jail and focus on the claims of a Steven Unruh about his alleged predawn interactions with the new inmate. Unruh, who had a history of theft and drug charges, told the weekly that he was being held in the cell next to Holmes and that Holmes had tried to harm himself—or end his life—by repeatedly bashing his head and body against a wall (those running the detention center quickly denied Unruh's story, but Unruh in turn disputed *them*).

According to Unruh, Holmes spent four hours yelling at him through cracks in the cell doors, saying that he'd been programmed to commit mass murder by an "evil therapist." Unruh further reported that Holmes said he "wasn't on his meds" and that during the shootings he felt "like he was in a video game." He stated that "nobody would help him" and mentioned a form of psychotherapy known as neuro-linguistic programming, which many in the psychiatric field had tried to discredit in recent years.

■ ■ ■

At seven a.m. on July 20, bomb technician Casey Overton climbed into a cherry picker outside Holmes's apartment building. As an officer covered him with a firearm, just in case someone was hiding inside Holmes's home, Overton was hoisted up to the apartment's bedroom, bathroom, and kitchen windows. The shades were pulled and the bedroom and bathroom lights were out, so he broke the glass in the bathroom. Using a wireless camera, Overton could only partially see within, making out a green ammunition can. He called for a lift truck to rip out the blinds and give him better sight lines.

By now, the Bureau of Alcohol, Tobacco, Firearms, and Explosives, the FBI, the Aurora Police Department, the Denver Bomb Unit, the Adams and Arapahoe County Bomb Units, and the Aurora Fire Department were all at the scene. The consensus was that attempting any other maneuvers without more knowledge of what was in the apartment would put too many lives at risk. Before doing anything else, they needed to speak to the person who'd built the IEDs: James Holmes himself. Even though several hours ago he'd asked for a lawyer, it was better to get to him now, before he actually had an attorney, and seek his help in defusing the apartment. Weren't the public safety issues more important than his Miranda rights? They all agreed that they had to talk with the suspect now in order to "make themselves smarter." Given the size of the operation, they needed all the intelligence they could gather.

In Holmes's car, an FBI agent had found an iPhone and passed it along to an Aurora police detective. He retrieved digital photos depicting Holmes right before the massacre and pulled up tracking data for a FedEx package. Three weeks earlier, on June 29, six boxes weighing a total of 170 pounds had been shipped from Atlanta to Aurora, arriving at Holmes's apartment four days later. The boxes came from a company called BulkAmmo.com and contained more than three thousand handgun rounds, three thousand rounds of .223-caliber rifle ammunition, and three hundred shotgun shells. Holmes had bought a second Glock and ordered a SWAT-style vest and magazine pouches from Tacticalgear.com.

As the bomb squad made plans to speak with Holmes at the jail, news of the shootings was spreading not just through Denver and the region, but across the nation and far beyond.

■ ■ ■

Just after dawn, the media contacted Arlene Holmes, a nurse living in a San Diego suburb, and asked if her son was the James Eagan Holmes who attended the Anschutz Campus at the University of Colorado. Startled by the question, she said yes and learned that the young man was in custody allegedly for mass murder. She immediately began searching for an attorney while the suspect's father, Dr. Robert Holmes, caught the first plane to Denver.

By mid-morning, Arlene had reached Iris Eyton, who worked in the Denver law office of Larry Posner, a well-known local defense attorney. Iris called the Aurora County Jail and said that she represented Holmes, but was told that for now no one was allowed to see him.

A few hours earlier, when APD Detective Craig Appel had briefly and frustratingly tried to interrogate Holmes, he'd told himself that he felt very sorry for the individual who'd eventually be put in charge of this massive investigation. Then he received a call from the police brass telling him that *he'd* been chosen to oversee the Aurora theater case.

One of his first duties as commander was to call Iris Eyton and inform her that the authorities were getting a search warrant from a judge so they could talk with Holmes in greater depth—*without* his lawyer present. Eyton wasn't happy about this, but Appel was unbending. Extreme public safety issues were in play, and the order to interview Holmes as soon as possible had come down from the head of the FBI in Washington, Robert Mueller.

The Denver Public Defender's office had already become involved in the case, and Chief Public Defender Daniel King and his investigator, John Gonglach, wanted to meet with Holmes, but they too were being kept at bay.

At 3:30 that afternoon, Appel and FBI Special Agent Bomb Technician Garrett Gumbinner sat down with Holmes, dressed in an orange jump and shackles. They did not re-inform him of his right to remain silent or of his right to an attorney but did say that in all their years in law enforcement, they'd never seen anything like his apartment and needed his assistance to prevent more destruction.

Was he willing to help them?

Holmes had come down from his playful mood and interrogation-room antics, no longer smirking or making hand puppets. He looked extremely tired and was very soft-spoken, but lucid. He talked with the men for thirty-eight minutes, describing the workings of the pyrotechnic firing box on his refrigerator and a remote-control detonating device that he'd planted outside his apartment building.

Like Holmes, Appel was emotionally drained and exhausted from not sleeping the night before—so tired that he forgot to turn on his tape recorder and half of the interview was lost.

They asked the suspect about the black shells and white powder inside his living space, about the three fusing systems they'd spotted with the robotic camera, and about some propane tanks.

Holmes said that once he'd left for the theater, a boom box inside his living room had been programmed for forty minutes of silence. At one a.m., it would start playing very loud music—so loud it would be heard throughout his building. He'd hoped to bring someone to his front door who'd push it open, trip the wires, trigger the IEDs, and demolish the entire structure.

Neither the detectives nor Holmes knew that one of his downstairs neighbors had heard the pounding music, angrily walked upstairs, and stood outside the door at a little after one a.m. Her hand was inches away from pulling the knob and tripping the wire, setting off a chain reaction that would level the building and send ripples of destruction up and down the block. She noticed that the door was ajar, striking her as suspicious, and returned to her apartment to call in a noise complaint to the police.

■ ■ ■

Should the authorities, Holmes was asked, evacuate other nearby apartment complexes?

No, he said, while calmly and methodically detailing the more than thirty homemade grenades, ten gallons of gasoline, and other explosives he'd built. During the thirty-eight minutes of conversation, he told the men precisely how to defuse the bombs. They thanked him, and he was taken back to his cell. His information would prove to be both accurate and invaluable.

The rest of that Friday, the Denver Public Defender's office continued trying to reach the suspect, but their requests were denied. Holmes's defense team would later claim that the police had deliberately misled them about where he was being held so that their time and efforts had been wasted in hunting for him at one correctional facility after another.

"Counsel spent the entire day attempting to locate and consult with Mr. Holmes," they wrote in a motion, "but were actively, improperly, and unconstitutionally rebuffed by law enforcement."

Because of this, the defense contended, all the information obtained in the inmate's discussion with Appel and Gumbinner, and the materials later recovered from his apartment, had been "involuntarily" gathered. Therefore, none of the statements or other evidence could be used against Holmes, since he'd already requested an attorney but not been provided one. Over the coming weekend, he finally was able to meet with a public defender, who outlined what would happen at his first court appearance on Monday morning, July 23.

■　■　■

No major crime in twenty-first-century America was complete without being surrounded by instant speculation on the Internet, much of which ran counter to the mainstream coverage of the event. Almost as soon as Holmes was booked, cyberspace began to cook with theories about what had *really* happened at the movie complex.

On August 1, 2012, a freelance writer from New York City named Jerry Mazza began trying to connect the dots around Holmes's family, his educational background, and his dark evolution into a mass shooter. Mazza posted an article called "James Holmes had Links to DARPA, the Salk Institute, and the DoD (Department of Defense)."

During the premiere showing of *The Dark Knight Rises* in Aurora, he wrote, a man dressed all in black and wearing a gas mask suddenly appeared at the front of the theater. After tossing several gas grenades, he opened fire with a forty-millimeter Glock, a 12-gauge shotgun, an AR-15 assault rifle with a 100-round drum magazine, and six thousand rounds of ammunition. A second Glock lay on his car seat.

Mazza described Holmes as a twenty-four-year-old neuroscience doctoral candidate with links to the Salk Institute, which was "involved in neurologically enhancing soldiers' abilities on the battlefield, and with connections to DARPA (Defense Advanced Research Projects Agency), the central research and development organization for the United States Department of Defense . . ."

A few years before the massacre, Mazza wrote, Holmes had worked at the Salk Institute, which had partnered with DARPA and the Mars Company (manufacturers of Milky Way and Snickers bars) to deter fatigue in combat troops through the enhanced use of epicatechina, found in cocoa and dark chocolate.

"The research," Mazza contended, "was part of a larger DARPA program known as the 'Peak Soldier Performance Program,' which involved *creating brain-machine interfaces* for battlefield use, including *human-robotic bionics for legs, arms, and eyes . . .*"

Like others posting their findings online, Mazza had looked into the Holmes family. According to his LinkedIn profile, James Holmes's father, Dr. Robert Holmes, worked for San Diego–based HNC Software, Inc., from 2000 to 2002: "HNC," Mazza wrote, "known as a 'neural network' company, and DARPA, beginning in 1998, have worked on developing 'cortronic neural networks,' which would *allow machines to interpret aural and visual stimuli to think like humans,* something you might find in the Batman epic."

Mazza wouldn't be the first or last commentator to compare what had happened inside Theater Nine to a fictional plot in a Robert Ludlum novel: "The links between the younger and elder Holmes and U.S. government research on creating super-soldiers, human brain-machine interfaces, and human-like robots brings forth the question: Was James Holmes engaged in a real-life Jason Bourne TREADSTONE project that broke down and resulted in deadly consequences in Aurora, Colorado?"

From a twenty-three-year-old male working in the food industry:

> *Young people have these conspiracy theories around cases like James Holmes because we don't really want to believe that others would do such things, or do them willingly. It's easier to think that someone was set up by some outside dark force than to look at these events and say, "What are they telling us about what's out of whack in the society? What are they saying about our emotional reality? What's standing in the way of social progress? What doesn't work anymore so that we can look at it and get rid of it now?"*

Interlude

In the late summer of 1998, when our son Eric had just turned five, we dropped him off at kindergarten for the first time, a few blocks from our home. Joyce had struggled with whether sending Eric to a private or a public school. For thirteen years, she'd attended Catholic schools, and she felt that he might get a better education at a private institution, but after researching the best public schools in our neighborhood, we ultimately picked one of them.

We never forgot taking him to kindergarten on that first morning and watching him line up on the sidewalk with the other kids and walk into the school, becoming absorbed into a group of boys and girls his own age. The experience was accompanied by a twinge of something a little unsettling. It wasn't just a matter of letting go of a measure of control over our child, which was normal and inevitable. But he was also entering a school system and joining a culture that we had little ability to influence. All we could do was hope that it was moving in the right direction, but a lot of evidence suggested otherwise.

One afternoon right after he entered kindergarten, at the height of the television coverage of the Monica Lewinsky/President Clinton sex scandal, we were in the living room with Eric. He was sitting on the floor drawing a picture of an animal.

He stopped and looked up at us.

"I hate the president," he said.

We glanced at each other and asked him what he meant.

"I hate the president," he said again.

As a five-year-old in kindergarten, he'd somehow picked up enough of the fallout from the scandal to start aping parts of the adult world, which had regularly been repeating their hatred of Bill Clinton.

We tried to counter what he was saying, but it's hard to convey the complexities of grown-up reality to a small child. If we could have taught him one thing, it would have been not to hate others, especially for their intimate behaviors, but he was already being shaped by other forces. He didn't pick up this view of the president from his mother or father because we didn't talk about hating Bill Clinton. He'd downloaded it from the environment he was growing up in—a media and political environment that was looking for the easy kill.

Eight months later in April 1999, the massacre at Columbine erupted in Denver. It followed some other school shootings—in Mississippi, Arkansas, Oregon, and elsewhere—but Columbine was especially horrific and occurred just a few miles away from where we lived. The reports coming out of the school after the tragedy reflected the larger social environment.

"Everyone hates you," Brooks Brown, a former student at Columbine, said about the school on Oprah Winfrey's afternoon TV show. Brown was referring to the cliques that had tormented him and other kids. "The people who made fun of me my whole life are still on top."

"It was relentless," Debra Sears told the *Rocky Mountain News* when describing the bullying at Columbine. In the mid-1990s, Sears had withdrawn her stepsons from the school because of the harassment: "The constant threats walking through the halls. You had a whole legion of people that would tell you that just going to school was unbearable."

"If you don't fit in at Columbine," Paula Reed, a teacher at the high school, told Oprah, "it gives you no options."

One of the counselors for the Columbine survivors and the victims' families was Dr. Frank Ochberg, a Michigan psychiatrist specializing in post-traumatic stress. He was brought to the school to help those suffering from nightmares and flashbacks. Referring to the shooters, Eric Harris and Dylan Klebold, Dr. Ochberg used a term employed by law enforcement and mental health experts when trying to identify dangerous students or others before they become murderers.

The term is "leakage," which means that signs of trouble or potential violence can leak out of kids as warning signals in advance of bloodshed. Experts have been trained to be on the lookout for leakage from such individuals. Dr. Ochberg indicated that there may have been some minor examples of leakage from Harris and Klebold before the massacre   signs that, unfortunately, no one in a position of authority had been astute enough to perceive or act on.

What wasn't focused on following Columbine was the concept of leakage in a whole society or how a bitterly divisive media, hate-saturated websites, violence-filled movies, and the widespread dynamics of demonization could have played a role in the development of these killers. The experts tended to look at the shootings more narrowly, searching for emotional problems or genetic defects or subtle brain dysfunctions that had gone undetected in individuals. They were attempting to pinpoint an organic personal flaw, not a social or cultural one.

According to Dr. Ochberg, Eric Harris was simply the "Mozart of psychopaths, the kind of person who comes along only every two or three hundred years."

Except that in the next fifteen years, in schools from coast to coast, and in malls and theaters and at other venues, this same "Mozart" kept appearing and reappearing with increasingly frequency—until mass shootings were being called an "epidemic."

Eric Harris was everywhere.

The difficulty, at least for some parents raising children and especially boys at the end of the 1990s, was that they were confronted with a dilemma that offered up no easy solutions. What they were trying to teach at home and what many young people were absorbing from the political and cultural realms were at striking odds—a gap that only got bigger with the arrival of the new millennium.

In addition to the effects of this surrounding environment, by the late nineties technology and social media were exploding, and no one could predict the impact this would have on the upcoming generation.

■ ■ ■

Following the shootings in Aurora, Eric looked back on his own formative years from a college perspective.

"Once you enter the school system," he told us, "the new 'parent' of the child is the culture. That includes other kids and their families, teachers, bureaucracy, entertainment, media, etcetera."

From the beginning in our household, Joyce had been adamant about not allowing Eric to purchase or play games that depicted murder. But that didn't mean he wasn't exposed to them.

"The minute you leave home," he said, "movies and video games become major influences because you're around other kids who are playing violent games. In ones like *Super Smash Brothers*, which was made for kids and families to play together, the characters are beating the hell out of each other. There's no visible blood or pain, but that's still the object of the game. Everyone was playing it when I was six or so."

It had taken fifteen years and the tragedy in Aurora before Eric really started talking with us about us how he grew up. He spoke about seemingly small things and things that weren't so small, things that were foundational to his youth. He filled in some of the gaps from all those times when he was silent.

"When *you* were young," he said to us, "the spheres of influence were much less, but technology has changed exponentially. Marketers know how to get young kids hooked on these games at a very early age. Millions of us were playing Pokémon, Yu-Gi-Oh!, Game Boys, and we were trading cards related to these games. Some young adults

I know are still playing them. You can get addicted to this, and it stays with you for the rest of your life, but it isn't attached to anything real.

"A baseball card, which was something you traded when you were young, was at least attached to something real: baseball itself. This other stuff isn't, and at age five you become a consumer. As you get older, you want to keep consuming. The games become much more violent and much more graphic, especially as the technology gets better. This was the starting point for a lot of boys my age."

He talked about making the transition from kindergarten to elementary school to middle school to high school.

"In elementary school," he said, "everything seems kind of equal with the kids. In middle school, the disparity is more evident. Some people appear to be more 'special' because of popularity or wearing the right sports clothing or their parents have a lot of money and status or whatever. In high school, most of us find coping mechanisms. 'How was school today?' your parents ask you. 'All right,' you say and you don't say anything else.

"You don't tell them. You never tell them. You try to protect your parents from what you're going through. Maybe you tell your friends. But some kids don't find good friends or good coping mechanisms. I was lucky. I found good friends. We understood why we didn't hang out with certain people. We understood boundaries.

"The thing about being that age is that it's all emotional. You can't talk about it. You just feel it all the time. Nobody teaches you how to deal with these feelings. School doesn't do that and the culture doesn't, either. School teaches you algebra, not how to live with your emotions. If your parents don't help you with this, what else is there? Some kids don't know how to cope with this.

"The school shooters are the ones who believe that they're not 'special.' There's something wrong with you. There's something missing."

THE SIXTH FLOOR

V

A Subway sandwich bag swung from the handlebars of his BMX bicycle, not quite big enough for his lanky frame, as he crossed Peoria Street and rode toward the Anschutz Medical Center. The June sky was sunny and warm, with pedestrians dressed casually in shirtsleeves and shorts on a perfect late-spring day in Aurora. James Holmes was in the process of severing his ties to the prestigious graduate program he'd entered the previous year.

He owned a car, the white Hyundai, but it was much easier to ride his bike the few hundred yards from his apartment on the west side of Peoria to the Center for Neuroscience on the east side. The Center was part of the new Anschutz campus, holding 3,100 postgrad candidates, six professional schools, and the University of Colorado Hospital, which billed itself as the "world's only completely new education, research, and patient care facility."

Denver's Philip Anschutz, a conservative Christian prominent in the Republican Party, was an oil and railroad tycoon before branching out into the media business. He owned *The Examiner* newspaper chain, the neoconservative *Weekly Standard*, and the Anschutz Entertainment Group (AEG), one of the world's largest sports and entertainment companies. In October 2010, *Forbes* magazine ranked him as the thirty-fourth-wealthiest person in America, worth an estimated $7 billion. He quietly and modestly contributed to charitable causes and to individuals in need, but the Anschutz campus wasn't modest at all.

His foundation had given a $91 million grant to help finance the new Medical Center, 577 acres that had once housed Fitzsimons Army Hospital. An elegant mixture of new glass-and-steel structures, the Center rose above manicured lawns featuring large, whimsical sculptures. The east side of Peoria Street conveyed money, privilege, and careers in research and academia, while the west side featured weathered bungalows with tattered roofs, gritty taverns, gang members, cheap restaurants, and the down-at-heels aura of a struggling neighborhood. Crossing Peoria, one could feel a dramatic shift in possibilities and hope.

Holmes had worked hard to earn that hope. By his early twenties, he had done everything he could to place himself on the path to academic and financial success. Throughout his earlier education, he'd been well liked and much admired for his achievements, the definition of a young man in pursuit of the American Dream. In March 2011, Holmes had been admitted to the CU neuroscience program and given a $26,000 grant from the National Institutes of Health, one of only six students accepted for the coming year. That May, he'd moved to Aurora and the following month he'd begun classes and lab rotations, drawing very little attention to himself.

On September 18, he e-mailed a CU Department of Psychiatry researcher who did brain scans and functional magnetic resonance imaging—fMRI—to study people with schizophrenia.

"The fmri study," he wrote the researcher, "sounds interesting and I would like to be a subject if possible. Cheers, James Holmes."

When the researcher responded with a schedule for the tests, he wrote back, "Ah, I can't make any of those times, best of luck."

On October 28, Holmes was ticketed for driving 46 mph in a 35 mph zone, his first-ever run-in with the law.

As a grad student, he was given a key card allowing him access to areas forbidden to civilians, including the sixth floor of the neuroscience building. Card in hand, he passed through a security door and entered a vast, gleaming, state-of-the art laboratory that stretched for hundreds and hundreds of feet, from one end of the structure to the other. Test tubes, vials, fuel tanks, refrigerators, laptop computers, electron microscopes that could enlarge objects four hundred times, "Radioactive Material," and the brains of fruit flies abounded. Students sat quietly in front of their screens, probing the wiring and synaptic firings of the brain and its connections to nerves, muscles, cells, molecules, and intestines. Holmes regularly huddled next to this elite group but rarely interacted with them.

In both labs and classrooms, he stood out for his silence and quirky sense of humor, giving one- or two-word responses to questions from professors or just nodding and smiling and saying, "Yo." He was physically quiet too, slinking off to study or eat alone, his five-foot-eleven-inch frame gliding out the door and down the hallway with barely a rustle. If he thought that he might have schizophrenia, or if he felt that he was drifting toward something dangerous, he mentioned this to no one.

At age twenty-four, he wasn't on Facebook, didn't e-mail or text much, and had a very outdated page on MySpace—as elusive online as he was in person. He'd done just about everything to remain anonymous, slipping quietly through the American educational landscape.

■ ■ ■

He wasn't as invisible as a youngster in Castroville in Northern California, the small farming community that he has referred to as "The Artichoke Center of the World." He had to wear a uniform to school every day, he once wrote in an application to graduate school at the University of Kansas, "to curb gang rivalry." Looking back on his early years and devotion to science, he explained that "my life could have gone in a completely different direction had I not possessed the foresight to choose the path of knowledge."

Holmes remained rather outgoing after his family relocated to Southern California, in the San Diego suburb of Rancho Penasquitos. His mother was a registered nurse and his father a leading scientist with the American credit score company FICO, previously known as Fair, Isaac and Company. James was a highly imaginative child whose natural inclination was to explore the furthest corners of his mind. His parents were more practical people who didn't always understand their son's flights of fancy. He could escape into his fantasy mind and stay there until something, or someone, brought him out of it.

At Westview High, he played soccer and ran cross-country. He liked to make other kids laugh with his improvisations and ad-libbing routines, but as he went deeper into science and the mysteries of the brain, he became more interior. He wanted to penetrate the secrets of the waking world, the dream world, and the mind—starting with his own. He wasn't that close to anyone, including his younger sister, Chris, a short-haired musician who resembled her brother.

People intrigued Holmes less than his own mental excursions. From puberty onward, he was captivated by the notion of being able to create one's reality using just the mind, and he was drawn to subjects like perceptual/temporal illusions and bending time. Science was clean and gave solid answers to complex problems.

Much later, when those from his past recalled Holmes, they spoke of him as a vague memory, a fleeting presence, a wisp of a young man who wasn't intimate with anyone—a trace of a person always on the move. Most could barely remember anything he'd said and not much that he'd done, not those in Castroville or those at Westview High or those at the University of California-Riverside, where he earned his undergraduate degree, or even those more recently at the Anschutz campus in Aurora.

Everybody conceded how bright he was. On the Anschutz campus, he'd critiqued other students' papers at a higher level than anyone else in the program. CU had turned down scores of other applicants, but Holmes's credentials were sterling, at the "top of the top" of his class. After winning a merit scholarship to UC-Riverside, he'd graduated in June 2010 as an honors student, earning a 3.94 grade point average. In a philosophy class titled "Ethics and the Meaning of Life," taken in the winter of 2010, he got an A. He was a member of Phi Beta Kappa, with Graduate Record Exam verbal scores in the ninety-eighth percentile. Leaving UC-Riverside, he'd worked briefly at a fast food restaurant while seeking out a graduate neuroscience program. A trio of UC-Riverside staff members wrote letters on his behalf, including director of student affairs Kathryn Jones and professors Khaleel Razak and Edward Korzus.

In one letter of recommendation penned by an unidentified author, Holmes was described as "truly exceptional."

Another letter read, "James is an extraordinarily gifted student who is very dedicated to his academic pursuits. He takes an active role in his education, and brings a great amount of intellectual and emotional maturity into the classroom. He is passionate about a career in science and seeks out opportunities to learn as much as possible about his chosen field of interest, and how he can positively contribute to the world."

His command of language was on display in his own applications.

"Rational people," he'd written, "act based on incentives for self-fulfillment, including fulfilling needs of self-development and needs of feeling useful and helpful to others . . . I look forward to fulfilling my quest to advance my knowledge, and I plan to use my critical thinking skills by studying the subject I am passionate about, neuroscience."

He had an "unquenchable curiosity, a strong desire to know and explore the unknown, and a need to persist against the odds . . . I have always been fascinated by the complexities of long lost thought seemingly arising out of nowhere into a stream of awareness. These fascinations likely stemmed from my interest in puzzles and paradoxes as an adolescent and continued through my curiosity in academic research . . .

"These are the very cognitive processes which enable us to acquire information and retain it. They are at the core of what distinguishes us as people. Due to the seemingly infinite vastness of indefinite knowledge, we must be selective in our pursuits of knowledge. This is why I have chosen to study the primary source of all things, our own minds . . . My lifelong goal is to increase the efficiency of how human beings learn and remember."

In his applications, he wrote about being a summer camp counselor and working with a dozen ten- and eleven-year-olds. Two of them had attention deficit disorder and another had schizophrenia. One night the latter child awoke at 3:30 a.m. and began vacuuming the ceiling of their cabin.

"These kids were heavily medicated," he recollected, using words that years later would eerily evoke his own case, "but this did not solve their problems. The medication changed them from being highly energetic creative kids to lax beings who slept through the activities."

In applying to the University of Alabama-Birmingham, he wrote an essay about his research into "the illusion between cause and effect relationships." He talked about a high school project and how he'd created an illusion in which "the mind is actually tricked into believing an action precedes the event that caused it."

A professor on the admissions committee at UAB had some concerns and wrote of Holmes, "Not sure. He may be extremely smart, but difficult to engage. Hard to tell how interested he is. Maybe he just wasn't interested in my research."

The interviewer had ranked Holmes a "4" on a scale of "1 to 5" and said that he had an "ability to describe research experience with clarity and depth." He gave Holmes a "3" in having clear goals and a "5" in research background.

Another UAB member of the admissions committee rated Holmes a "5" in all five categories, saying, "Excellent applicant! Great GPA and GRE scores."

A third UAB interviewer dismissed Holmes's introverted nature as being problematic: "His personality may not be as engaging as some applicants, but he is going to be a leader in the future."

Despite the good reviews, UAB told Holmes that many "well qualified students applied, which forced the admissions committee to make difficult decisions. We regret to inform you that you have not been recommended for admission."

■ ■ ■

Others schools were more welcoming. The University of Kansas offered him an interview, but then he withdrew his application. In early 2011, the University of Illinois accepted Holmes with this comment, "Those who met you . . . during your interview visit felt that your personal and professional qualities are truly outstanding and that you will be an excellent match for our program."

But on January 30 of that year, Daniel Tranel, the neuroscience program director at the University of Iowa and the head of the grad school admissions committee, sent a stark e-mail to his colleagues about seven "applicants from this past weekend." Six of the seven were described with words like "stellar" or "solid, not spectacular." Only one candidate was dismissed outright: James Holmes. After meeting with Holmes, Tranel urged the admissions committee to reject his application.

"Do NOT," he wrote, "offer admission under any circumstances," but he did not explain the reasons for taking this position. Nor would he comment later on why he'd reached this conclusion.

Mark Blumberg, also on the Iowa faculty, wrote in an e-mail, "James Holmes: I agree with Dan. Don't admit."

So he did not receive acceptance to the University of Iowa. With schools in Kansas, Iowa, and Alabama out of the running, he chose the University of Colorado over Illinois and made plans to move to Aurora, finding an apartment just two blocks from the Anschutz campus and four miles from the Century 16 movie complex in Aurora.

From a twenty-nine-year-old male in medical school:

If I had a magic wand, the first thing I'd do is try to make myself better, instead of fixing the world around me. We act out of fear way too often instead of acting out of love. If I could change that within myself, then maybe I could believe that others can do this too. Who knows how something like that small shift inside might have helped James Holmes? What keeps people from going insane are the tiny things—regular contact with people, making music with friends, or being a little bit more understanding of others. It's the absence of all these things in Holmes's life that's most revealing. Fear controls everything and most everyone—the fear of making yourself vulnerable and of being exposed, the fear of coming out of your isolation and taking a chance with someone else. You can't really know who you are until someone has taken a good hard look at you and told you the truth about yourself, but you have to be willing to go through this process with another human being. Or you can stay hidden.

VI

He'd hardly been accepted into the Anschutz academic community without scrutiny. Each year about thirty to forty undergraduates applied to the CU Neuroscience Program with a dozen or so brought in to be interviewed for the openings. Of this group, usually four to six were chosen for that fall's entering class. An applicant went through a routine background check for illegal activities and might be interviewed and screened by as many as eight faculty members. Entering the program, the grad student was paired with a mentor whose specialty was often in the branch of neuroscience the PhD candidate was most interested in. He or she initially took elective courses with overviews of cellular and molecular biology and various mental disorders. The candidate also had a series of laboratory rotations, working with three doctors and spending about ten weeks on miniature projects. Students were observed for unusual behaviors or high levels of stress and kept under what one professor has called "a fair amount of oversight." Therapy was available, but serious problems were rare. In the past, one PhD candidate had simply vanished for a while, before showing up alive in another location.

"The stress level that first year," says a member of the Anschutz faculty, "is moderate for most students. In the case of James Holmes, nobody on the staff felt that he was under excessive pressure or brought it up in meetings. No one was waving red flags."

During the 2011–12 school year, Holmes studied the human auditory system in the lab of Dr. Achim Klug; the "messenger" chemicals in the brain with Dr. Curt Freed; and synaptic signaling with Dr. Mark Dell'Acqua. The young man was on track to succeed in one of science's most advanced fields. Physicians were using neuroscience to isolate which parts of the brain control which movements of different appendages of the body. The possibilities were stunning. Paraplegics whose brains were intact, for example, could now successfully employ robotic arms, hands, and fingers—by simply *thinking* about what a hand can do and then transmitting that thought electronically to the robot. The mechanical hand reached out and retrieved a cup of tea or a cookie and brought it up to one's mouth.

Neuroscience could penetrate the deepest physical secrets of the brain, but did it have anything to say about emotional stability?

"In early 2012, after James had been in the program for about six months, I heard him give an oral presentation," says a professor at Anschutz. "I was really quite impressed. It was about the nervous system of lobsters and about how the neurons connect to the nerve cells and how this creates behavior in the lobster's stomach. Holmes had clearly done his homework and was good at conducting complex scientific experiments and analyzing data. He knew how to read scientific papers and how to talk about them.

"It isn't enough in grad school just to be able to do research or even to write a good paper. You also have to know how to present your information clearly to an audience, and Holmes did. His presentation was really excellent. He was probably already thinking about what he was going to do, but he was still able to compartmentalize everything in his life.

"What I remember most was his odd sense of humor when speaking in public. It wasn't dark, really, just strange. I tried to explain this to a detective when he came to the school to speak with us, but it was hard to put into words. His sense of humor was odd, but not that odd. You've got to remember that many gifted scientists are quirky, so his behavior didn't stand out here. You can get away with being quirky, if you're good enough at what you do."

■ ■ ■

Off campus, Holmes said little to those at the Laundromat, the pawnshop, the liquor store, or the discount ethnic outlet, MexMall, where he went shopping. At night, he sat by himself in Shepes Rincon, the Spanish-speaking bar across from his apartment, sipping beers and saying almost nothing to the other patrons. After emptying three or four bottles, according to later accounts from people at the bar, he slid off his stool and headed home. Some evenings, he played video games or surfed adult sites on the Internet. Other times he met up with a prostitute in a brothel or had one entertain him in his own bedroom. He always had in hand the $240 cash for this service. He didn't talk much to the call girls, either, or tell them anything about his dreams or violent fantasies. He could be gentle but suddenly turn rough, painfully twisting their hands or wrists, giving the impression that he didn't understand they were suffering.

As he drank at Shepes or had sexual encounters, he didn't talk about the movies he'd been watching obsessively, or the materials he was having delivered to his apartment, or about checking out firing ranges in the Denver area for target practice. One gun range owner, Glenn Rotkovich, had recently received an e-mail from Holmes asking to apply for membership at his place of business. Rotkovich called him back, and Holmes's returned the call, leaving a bizarre, Batman-style voicemail. Rotkovich felt unnerved by the message. If the young man showed up at the club, Rotkovich warned his staff, don't let him in.

Holmes didn't talk to anyone about what he was imagining or feeling—not his parents, sister, classmates, or other acquaintances. He didn't have any close friends at the campus and didn't reveal to his teachers or his CU mentor what he'd been thinking or learning about mental disorders. He didn't let anyone know about his growing interest in guns or that for months he'd been keeping a detailed, one-hundred-page brown spiral notebook holding his most private thoughts and desires. He liked to write and draw stick figures who acted out his deepest visions. The notebook, entitled "Of Life," was decorated with an infinity symbol. Because he had trouble speaking with others, he used these pages to carry on a conversation with himself, sliding further and further into the realm of make-believe.

An unseen line, nothing like the tangible strip of pavement that separated the wealth on the east side of Peoria Street from the relative poverty on the west side, stood between the world of academia Holmes had been living in and the world he was now entering. He was developing a secret identity, dressing up like Batman in his apartment and slipping black contact lenses into his eyes, as revealed later at his preliminary hearing. He was planning on dying his hair orange, the color of The Joker's. He'd once thought about working for the U.S. military and using his neuroscience insights and techniques to interrogate prisoners of war in places like Iraq or Afghanistan. He was certain that he knew how to get information out of people that no one else could. Weren't you supposed to identify evil and stamp it out? Wasn't that how you might become revered as a hero? His only connection to the world of warfare now, as for so many of his generation, came when he was playing video games by himself.

The professors at the CU Neuroscience Program had all studied the brain and the central nervous system and knew everything about neurons and proteins, but they had no concept of what was moving through his brain and nerves. They saw only the surface—his little smiles and friendly nods as he passed them in the hallways and kept moving. Holmes knew they'd interpret him as harmless. Even the name he'd given himself on campus, "Jimmy James," was innocuous.

He only made one shocking admission, in March 2012, nine months after starting the PhD program and about four months before the Aurora theater massacre, telling a fellow student that he wanted to kill people "when my life is over." But nobody followed up on this remark or knew that when he left the campus, he drove around greater Denver, scouring the city and the suburbs for guns. He studied Glocks at the Gander Mountain outlet in Aurora; looked at Remington 12-gauge shotguns at Bass Pro Shops in Denver; and handled the Smith & Wesson AR-15 semiautomatic rifles at Gander Mountain in Thornton. He constantly went online searching for gear—combat vests, magazine holders, and knives—paying extra for the two-day shipping.

From a twenty-four-year-old male in Wisconsin:

> Why is violence such a large part of our entertainment culture? Because it's so profitable. When I was ten, we were all playing less graphic video games, but as you get older, the companies you buy the games from start to make them more and more graphic and violent. Call of Duty is one of the most popular games of all time. When you're playing it, you become the figure in the game who wakes up in a drugged-out state. You don't know where you are. You're an assassin who's been neuro-linguistically programmed to kill President Kennedy.
>
> These games are what countless young males get for Christmas now. They wake up that morning, open their presents, and start playing this game with other kids—killing people all over the world in these videos. It's how they celebrate what's supposed to be America's biggest and most sacred holiday. Is this escapist? Sure. Is it desensitizing? Absolutely. Does it reward you for creating as much chaos as possible? Yep. It is fun to play and beat others? No doubt.
>
> When I was in college, my roommates would come home from class and sit down and play the games for two or three straight hours. They weren't young teenagers anymore. They were in their twenties and studying to be doctors and engineers, but this is still how they relaxed.

VII

Part of the changes within himself that Holmes recorded in his spiral notebook resulted from taking drugs. He was on numerous prescription medications and had told someone later interviewed by the *New York Times* in October 2012 that he'd experimented with hallucinogens, including LSD (in October 2014 CNN's Ivan Watson reported that someone else who'd recently been violent, a nineteen-year-old rebel fighter named Kareem, fighting for the Islamic militant group ISIS, was given hallucinogenic drugs before going into battle so that he'd be indifferent to whether he lived or died).

In 1938, Dr. Albert Hofman had synthesized lysergic acid diethylamine—two thousand times stronger than any known psychoactive drug in the United States. Most of the LSD research carried out over the next three decades was funded by the federal government and undertaken within the Army Chemical Corps and the CIA's Technical Services branch, in programs like "Project MK ULTRA." Experiments were done on animals and humans until the substance was finally outlawed in 1968, but people had never stopped making and taking it on their own.

Holmes had read about Timothy Leary's research into LSD and psilocybin in the 1960s. Leary had been an accomplished clinical psychologist at Harvard before the university dismissed him for his experiments with psychedelic drugs. Researchers today know far more about the brain than when Leary was doing hallucinogens, and Holmes had absorbed some of that knowledge in class. He knew, for example, that the frontal lobe continued developing well into one's early twenties; it was still in a "plastic" state and not yet entirely formed. A recent National Institutes of Health study concluded that the part of the brain that limits risky behavior, like drinking and reckless driving, isn't completely developed until age twenty-five. Young adults have extra synapses in the areas where risk assessment and decision making occur, and these synapses can impair one's judgment.

Despite the enormous complexities of introducing artificial chemicals into the brain, Holmes was intrigued by what effects the drug might have on him. What could he learn from ingesting LSD that might be applicable or beneficial to his PhD work in neuroscience or even his future career? Would taking LSD give him insights his classmates didn't have and an edge in the classroom?

For years, he'd had a penchant for exploring alternative states of consciousness—wanting to tamper with the past or to alter time or to create reality with just his thoughts, as a paraplegic could now do with a robotic hand by merely thinking about something. Could Holmes go into other mental states or know the actual sensation of psychiatric disorders through artificial means? Could he find out what it felt like to be partially insane or schizophrenic by taking a drug? Grad students talked a lot about schizophrenia and other mental illnesses in the classroom, but what if he could experience a semblance of the disorder for himself?

"Most psychotropic stimulants work by mimicking or activating neuro-chemical pathways in the brain," says a CU professor of neuroscience, who like everyone else at the university had been placed under a gag order following the massacre. (He could only speak on the condition of anonymity and not about any of the specifics of the case.) "LSD can cross all the barriers in the mind and affect all of the chemistry. When this occurs, different circuits start to activate and to change. What's been under control within the brain and the emotions is no longer controlled. It's not true that there can't be long-term effects from this, but every individual responds differently. When you give cocaine to rats, you see permanent effects in their brains.

"The frontal lobe is one emotional center of the brain. It allows you to control and suppress anti-social impulses and behaviors. When you change the chemistry in the frontal lobe, as drugs do, it can alter the personality. This is why doctors used to do frontal lobotomies and why they were so popular for a while. Change the frontal lobe and you really can change someone's life.

"Some people in neuroscience programs have taken certain stimulants to learn more about them, but this has to be extremely well-controlled. Different drugs have very different effects on different people. There are cultures that use psychotropic drugs for ritualistic purposes, but they do so in a highly controlled environment. Without that, some people can get very sick on these drugs, and they can severely hallucinate, but other people are all right. We simply don't know enough to make accurate predictions about the consequences of doing these things.

"You can be sure that people in neuroscience have done their own experiments with lots of different drugs, legal and illegal, but they have to be aware of the dangers. In our department, we talk about these substances, and some students want to explore them, but there's no encouragement of this activity on the part of the faculty.

"It's just a hypothesis that taking LSD or a derivative would simulate the effects of schizophrenia. Yet it wouldn't shock me if these drugs are involved in this case. I have no idea what our students do when they leave the campus and go home in the evenings, but it would disappoint me if I felt they were doing this kind of experimentation by themselves. The brain is a fragile thing, especially when you're young.

"If you take LSD or a combination of anti-depressants and anti-anxiety drugs, or a combination of all of these, you're affecting multiple pathways in the brain. You can't predict what will happen or what the effects will be. Just because you're knowledgeable about how drugs work because you're in a PhD program doesn't mean that you're wise about making decisions.

"If a physician had prescribed Holmes drugs for depression or anxiety, that individual wouldn't really know what else he was taking, unless he told them, and that's unlikely if he was using illegal substances. There are some very dangerous drugs out there."

■ ■ ■

In the last week of August and the first week of September 2013, three young people in New York and Boston, along with a University of Virginia sophomore, all died from taking Molly (short for a pure "molecule" of Ecstasy, also known as MDMA). Then three more overdosed at a concert on the Boston waterfront. The authorities suspected that a single batch of the synthetic drug had caused these deaths, plus a dozen other overdoses that summer at a nightclub in the Boston suburb of Quincy. The University of Virginia victim, Mary "Shelley" Goldsmith, nineteen, an honors student and sorority member, had taken Molly at a rave concert earlier in the evening. Not just James Holmes, but his entire generation, was experimenting—or being experimented on—with a series of legal and illegal drugs whose immediate and long-term effects were unknown.

From a twenty-six-year-old male in south Texas:

> *People my age take a lot more drugs than you realize. We take a lot of prescription drugs, like Ritalin and Adderall, and a lot of recreational drugs, like pot and mushrooms and psychedelics. If you know something about expanding the mind, this can be a good experience. But if you don't, it can be very risky. If you do enough of these drugs, you can get too isolated and to the point where you can only talk to people who've done the same drugs.*

VIII

Holmes had also been impulsively watching *The Dark Knight* and in particular the character of The Joker, who stole every scene in the movie, partly because of his garish makeup and disheveled orange hair. Played by Australian actor Heath Ledger, The Joker was the film's most disturbing and provocative character. Utterly cynical and utterly destructive, he was deeply intelligent and insightful about the dynamics of human society (and about the human brain and emotions). Ledger's acting in the movie had made him a bigger star, especially among the young.

On January 22, 2008, a few months after completing the filming of *The Dark Knight*, the twenty-eight-year-old actor died from what the authorities called an accidental "intoxication from prescription drugs." Some who knew him and had observed him in recent months believed that taking on The Joker role had contributed to his downfall. In 1989, Jack Nicholson had played the same part in another Batman film. When he learned that Ledger was dead, he said to reporters in London, "Well, I warned him."

Ledger himself had told the press that he'd slept only two hours a night while playing "a psychopathic, mass-murdering, schizophrenic clown with zero empathy . . . I couldn't stop thinking. My body was exhausted, and my mind was still going."

The prescription drugs he'd taken had apparently neither helped him sleep nor calmed him down, and his death instantly set off endless speculation that he may have committed suicide because of his immersion into The Joker's unrelenting darkness. Fifteen days after his demise, the Office of the Chief Medical Examiner of New York released its findings.

"Heath Ledger," the report said, "died as the result of acute intoxication by the combined effects of oxycodone, hydrocodone, diazepam, temazepam, alprazolam, and doxylamine . . . We have concluded that the manner of death is accident, resulting from the abuse of prescription medications."

During the filming of the movie and leading up to his death, Ledger—like Holmes with his spiral notebook—kept an extensive diary about his experience playing The Joker. A series of drawings reflected the character's mindset, along with written entries, Batman comics, magazine clippings, and photos from the movie *A Clockwork Orange*. For weeks Ledger had locked himself in a hotel room in order to get into the mental and emotional reality of The Joker. Across one page of the diary, he'd scrawled, "Bye Bye."

The actor posthumously received numerous accolades for his work in the movie, including the Golden Globe and the Academy Award for Best Supporting Actor. He'd lent a twisted allure to a character that embodied violence, while he mocked just about everything in society that can be mocked. The filmgoing generation of teenagers and twentysomethings, including Holmes, had been raised under the near-constant threat of disaster in America and imminent collapse. Countless movies and TV programs aimed at them were dystopian, apocalyptic, or post-apocalyptic, populated by zombies, vampires, and huge mechanical monsters storming through cities and wreaking havoc.

Their generation had lived through nonstop media reports of impending doom with the arrival of the year 2000; through the September 11 attacks and the neverending broadcasts about terrorism striking the United States; through the subsequent eleven years of American warfare abroad and massive secretive domestic surveillance at home; through repeated warnings of disaster regarding global warming; through the economic chaos that had begun in 2008 and led to the Great Recession; through great fears from borrowing tens of thousands of dollars or more just to attend college and the accompanying fears of not being able to find a decent job once you graduate; and to the much reported Mayan prophesy that claimed the end of the world would arrive on December 21, 2012—four months after the shootings in Aurora. The date was considered by many as the end of a 5,126 year cycle in the Mesoamerican calendar and could therefore signal an unknown catastrophe. But before the date arrived, some Mayan scholars publicly said this was a misinterpretation of the astronomical calendar.

■ ■ ■

The Joker had given young moviegoers a focal point for hopelessness, an escape into violent fantasy, and a profound distrust of authority and the mainstream media. Ledger's character was by far the smartest, shrewdest, most powerful, and most manipulative in the film, the one in control of the plot. He acted—while everyone else *reacted* to him. He called the shots, then stood back and watched as others cleaned up the messes he'd left in his wake.

The Joker could easily appeal to someone with deep intellectual vanity, especially someone with exceptional mental gifts, but someone detached from other people and his own emotions. The Joker showed everyone in the movie and the audience just how effortlessly he could fool the system and create chaos, causing the population around him and the authority figures to become slaves to their own angers and fears. He wasn't part of a society or any of its rules. He loomed above it, beyond it, and took delight in making fun of the culture and the values it professed to believe in. He knew exactly how to control the synaptic firings and the adrenalin glands of those around him—without having to get a PhD in neuroscience.

The Joker was less a person than an idea and was incapable of feeling the consequences of his actions.

Holmes knew that by activating aspects of the brain or central nervous system, one could get people to buy what one wanted them to buy, feel what one wanted them to feel, think what one wanted them to think, and do whatever one wanted them to do. One could stimulate this set of neurons or depress that one and get just the response one was looking for—in fruit flies, lobsters, or human beings. One could get people to consume more of what one was selling or make soldiers in combat less fatigued on the battlefield or have them become less inhibited when it came to killing the enemy.

It was almost like becoming an action hero, while feeling nothing at all.

The Joker was invincible. He didn't die or suffer in any way for his destructive deeds. His goal was to have an effect on society—a very large effect that he could observe—and he followed his plans down to the last detail, always a step or two ahead of the authorities, creating mass horror and watching others pay for it.

He also had the best lines in the movie:

"Some men aren't looking for anything logical, like money. They can't be bought, bullied, reasoned, or negotiated with. Some men just want to watch the world burn."

"Look what I did to this city with a few drums of gas and a couple of bullets. I'm not a schemer. I'm trying to show the schemers just how pathetic their attempts to control things really are."

"I'm not a monster. I'm just ahead of the curve."

"Madness is like gravity. All it takes is a little push."

Something had recently given Holmes a little push, causing him to leap into a fictional realm and a comic-book life, making him more susceptible to the influences he'd long been surrounded by: the violent movies and video games he'd grown up with, including *Diablo III* and *World of Warcraft*. In 2009 on eBay, he'd purchased *Neverwinter Nights II*, a role-playing game like *Dungeons & Dragons*.

And in the spring of 2012 he was undergoing this transformation while in the care of one of the most qualified mental health experts on the Anschutz campus.

IX

Prior to 2005, Dr. Lynne Fenton had been in private practice in Physical Medicine and Rehabilitation. That year, she entered the psychiatry residency program at the University of Colorado-Denver. Because her test scores were high and her interpersonal skills were excellent, she became the chief resident at UCD. In 2009, she was hired as the director of the Anschutz Medical Campus mental health service for students, and the following year CU made her an associate professor of psychiatry. While earning around $150,000 a year, she taught classes, supervised residents, and became a research fellow with the Veterans Administration. Her specialty was, as she wrote in her online biography, "the neurobiology of psychotherapy, what happens in the brain with psychotherapy, and why does it work."

Each week Dr. Fenton met with ten to fifteen patients, all from the university, for medication and therapy. Schizophrenia was her primary research interest, just as Holmes himself had once worked with schizophrenic youngsters during a summer internship following high school—and just as in September 2011 he'd thought about working with a CU Department of Psychiatry researcher who did brain scans and functional magnetic resonance imaging to study people with schizophrenia.

On the Anschutz campus, Dr. Fenton trained students to recognize the oncoming signs of mental health problems and how to respond to them. Her care was campus-based and focused solely on the student population. Prevention was always the therapeutic goal—to stop a bad situation before it got worse. As part of her commitment to stay out in front of psychiatric troubles, she led the effort to create a campus-wide Behavioral Evaluation and Threat Assessment, or BETA, team. This group of administrators provided support, referrals, and information to those students dealing with threatening or disruptive situations. Her performance evaluations for 2010 and 2011 had called her "outstanding" and far exceeding "performance expectations."

What exactly Holmes had told her would, like the spiral notebook itself, be buried under a gag order that would go on for years. Because of this order and because Dr. Fenton had never openly or fully testified in court about these matters, we know only that he saw her on numerous occasions in the spring of 2012 and that their sessions ended in mid-June.

That spring Holmes began calling "Diggity" Dave Aragon, an actor from the MTV series *Pimp My Ride*. Aragon was the director of the low-budget film *Suffocator of Sins*, a tale of vigilante justice and over-the-top violence, and a dark reimagining of the Batman saga. On the phone with Aragon, Holmes identified himself by name and explained that he was enthralled with the movie's four-minute online trailer. He'd watched it repeatedly, pressing the director for more details about the complete film.

After the massacre, Aragon remembered the calls.

"He came off as articulate, nervous, on the meek side," Aragon told *The New York Times*. "He was obviously interested in the body count."

■ ■ ■

Around the same time that he was watching *The Dark Knight* and *Suffocator of Sins*, Holmes gave a presentation on MicroRNA Biomarkers in a class entitled the Biological Basis of Psychiatric and Neurological Disorders. His paper confronted the question of genes and heredity in mental illness and expanded on issues he'd been studying for the past half dozen years.

At eighteen, he'd done a six-week internship at the prestigious Salk Institute of Biology in Southern California. The Institute is considered one of the world's top biomedical research facilities: "a temple of science, a secular monastery where man pursues knowledge of our biological foundations."

At Salk, he was under the supervision of John Jacobsen, and in a video made during his internship, Holmes said, "Over the course of the summer I've been working on . . . an illusion that allows you to change the past . . . Subjective experience is what takes place inside the mind as opposed to the external world. I've carried on his [Jacobsen's] work in dealing with subjective experience."

Jacobson, who would instantly try to distance himself from Holmes following the massacre, had coauthored a paper with David Eagleman for the journal *Nature*. Eagleman was a PhD in the Departments of Neuroscience and Psychiatry at the Baylor College of Medicine in Houston. The "Eagleman Laboratory for Perception and Action" was funded by the National Institutes for Health and by DARPA, the part of the U.S. Department of Defense responsible for developing cutting-edge technology for use by the American military.

As part of his work, Eagleman had explored a subject that was becoming more and more prominent within both scientific circles and the American legal system: the role of genetics and the brain in criminal behavior. In the July/August 2011 issue of *The Atlantic*, he'd published "The Brain on Trial," just as Holmes was beginning his studies at CU.

"Human behavior," Eagleman summarized, "cannot be separated from human biology. If we like to believe that people make free choices about their behavior (as in, 'I don't gamble, because I'm strong-willed') . . . perhaps not everyone is equally 'free' to make socially appropriate choices . . . As our understanding of the human brain improves, juries are increasingly challenged with these sorts of questions. When a criminal stands in front of the judge's bench today, the legal system wants to know whether he is blameworthy. Was it his fault, or his biology's fault?"

Eagleman concluded, "Free will can at best be a small factor riding on top of vast neural networks shaped by genes and environment . . . A forward-thinking legal system will [view] criminal behavior the way we understand other medical conditions such as epilepsy, schizophrenia, and depression—conditions that now allow the seeking and giving of help."

Dr. Eagleman could never have imagined how these exact issues would one day play out in a suburban Denver courtroom, with a former Salk intern at the heart of them.

Says a CU professor who observed Holmes in the classroom, "I think there's a lot of hyperbole and false expectations around science and the law. We can do an MRI on the brain and look for certain things, but no one is close to saying that this is actually predictive of violent behavior. If you look at someone's brain five months after he's murdered someone, that doesn't tell you anything about what the brain was doing when these actions occurred. It's unlikely that such tests will be useful in court, unless there's something very obvious at work, like a growing tumor.

"What you can say is that the deaths in Aurora might have been prevented if it weren't so easy for someone like Holmes to get his hands on so many weapons."

■ ■ ■

That spring, as Holmes was meeting with Dr. Fenton, he displayed increasingly disturbing signs. His classroom performance was slipping from the previous winter, and he was watching violent video content and speaking with Dave Aragon about his fascination with

Sufficator of Sins. He was scouting gun stores and researching how to order ammunition online. On June 11, he met with Dr. Fenton for the last time and, according to a source in a December 2012 article in *The Denver Post,* he talked about having fantasies about killing "a lot of people." Court records show that in the part of Dr. Fenton's "Client Profile" for this session, the category labeled "Dangerousness" was blacked out, indicating that she had considered him dangerous. But we do not know to what degree, or how urgent and immediate, her concerns were for his well-being and the well-being of those around him.

We do know that Dr. Fenton decided not to hold him for the mandatory seventy-two-hour evaluation—the law in Colorado if a therapist feels that a patient is a danger to himself or the community (each year, the state sees about 2,800 of these holds). Since the 1976 *Tarasoff* ruling by the California Supreme Court, following the murder of UC Berkeley student Tatiana Tarasoff, psychiatrists could legally break patient confidentiality and divulge information on a patient if they believed he might harm others. In Colorado, therapists and their institutions are exempt from liability in civil actions for "failure to warn or protect any person against a mental health patient's violent behavior"—except when that patient has communicated a "serious threat of imminent physical violence against a specific person or persons"—which Holmes did according to the *Post* article.

After her final meeting with Holmes, a little more than a month before the massacre, Dr. Fenton contacted the campus Behavioral Evaluation and Threat Assessment (BETA) team. The next day Holmes's key card that allowed access to the CU buildings was deactivated, and he left the neuroscience program. Since he was no longer a student on the campus, BETA had stopped monitoring his movements (because of this, Chantel Blunk, the estranged wife of Jonathan Blunk, a forty-seven-year-old father of two who was killed in the shooting, would eventually sue CU and Dr. Fenton).

Holmes was now on his own—untethered from his research and his school and no longer under the care of a psychiatric professional. He was isolated to a degree he'd never been before in Aurora, if not in his whole life. The daily interactions with classmates and professors were gone, and he had no known social circle or close friends. His attachment to a normal routine had been severed.

From a twenty-five-year-old male graduate student:

> If you don't have close friends or a good relationship with your parents, what do you have? Action characters in video games and movies. The point of these games is violence.
>
> You learn to cope through fantasy games and drugs. Through some form of escape. I see this everywhere in people my age. They feel powerless. They have a lot of intelligence, just like James Holmes, but not a lot of tools for coping.
>
> The video games cover all the recent wars: Vietnam, Korea, Afghanistan, and Iraq. It's not hard to figure how someone raised on this stuff could act it out in a real way that causes real violence. Holmes's crime is exactly like something out of a video game. He's basically acting out something he's already seen in a fictional scene.

X

Following the Aurora theater shootings, the media seized on a June 7 oral exam that Holmes had performed poorly on as a possible catalyst for the massacre. Following this test, one of his professors had reportedly told him to seek another career. Later that same day, he'd bought an AR-15 assault rifle, and both the press and prosecutors tried to depict the botched exam as the catalytic event for his violence. But sixteen days before the test, on May 22, Holmes had purchased the first of two Glock pistols at Aurora's Gander Mountain gun shop. Six days after that, he'd bought a Remington 12-gauge shotgun at Denver's Bass Pro Shops—arming himself well before he took the exam. While visiting weapons stores and browsing among the firearms all through the spring of 2012, he'd gradually been drifting away from the CU neuroscience program.

"I saw James give a talk in mid-to-late May," says a professor at the Anschutz campus, "and it wasn't memorable at all. Several months earlier, when I'd watched him make another presentation, it was obvious to me that he'd put a lot of time and research into his work. He hadn't thought out this new one very well. I got the impression that he was no longer engaged in what he was doing or committed to his career. He wasn't sloppy, really. He just wasn't fully present.

"When he took the oral exam a couple of weeks later, he was asked how certain parts of the brain work and how cells communicate with one another. The test isn't designed to flunk people out of the program, but to see if they're competent and capable of going forward. If he'd been making progress in other things at school, he could have easily been given a second chance on this exam. It wasn't necessarily a terminal thing, but by then his classes and research weren't going well, either.

"Despite all this, nothing about him seemed that unusual, not even at that second presentation. It's very jarring to think back on this now. You have a qualified graduate student who's truly dangerous standing right in front of you—and you don't pick up on what's happening."

■ ■ ■

On June 10, three days after the oral exam, Holmes started the process of dropping out of school.

On June 11, he met with Dr. Fenton for the last time and told her about his violent fantasies.

On June 12, Dr. Fenton reached out to University of Colorado Police Officer Lynn Whitten, telling Officer Whitten that Holmes had stopped seeing her the day before. A search warrant in the case reads, "Dr. Fenton advised (Whitten) that through her contact with James Holmes she was reporting, per her requirement, his danger to the public due to homicidal statements he had made."

The Post reported that when Whitten asked Fenton if she should apprehend Holmes and place him on a mandatory seventy-two-hour psychiatric hold, the psychiatrist said no. It isn't clear if she rejected this offer because she didn't think Holmes was a danger to himself or the community—or because he was in the process of leaving the CU neuroscience graduate program and was no longer the university's responsibility. In late August 2012, Dr. Fenton made a brief appearance at a court hearing. She never explained in court or to the media about her decision not to place Holmes on psychiatric hold.

After Officer Whitten deactivated Holmes's keycard, CU denied that Holmes was banned from the campus for making threats, saying only that this deactivation was part of a normal process when a student withdraws from school.

On June 13, Holmes bought a 100-round magazine for his new AR-15-style rifle. Under a prior federal assault weapons ban, several versions of the AR-15 had been outlawed for civilian sale, but that statute had expired in 2004. All versions of this highly lethal weapon were now for sale within the United States (where there are eighty-eight guns for every 100 people; by contrast, Britain has six guns per 100 people).

Mass shootings that involve large-capacity gun magazines are significantly more deadly than those that do not, according to the non-profit Citizens Crime Commission of New York City. The Commission's "Mass Shooting Incidents in America" database catalogs shootings since 1984 that resulted in more than four deaths. Mass shootings, the database shows, were dramatically less deadly between 1994 and 2004, when the federal Assault Weapons Ban was in effect.

"The number of people killed or injured in mass shootings during the decade of the ban was half what it was in the decade before (119 v. 241)," researchers wrote. "And it was a third of the number of casualties since (329 from September 2004 through 2012)."

■ ■ ■

Holmes had access to a Platinum MasterCard, and on June 28, three weeks after failing his oral exam, he began placing orders for 6,300 rounds of ammunition to BulkAmmo.com. The online company, according to its website, offered "only the best deals to the most serious shooters for bulk handgun ammo, bulk rifle ammo, bulk shotgun ammo, and bulk rimfire ammo." Their AR-15 bullets had a special steel core, capable of blasting through, for example, theater seats and theater walls and hitting multiple victims with each round. In the past it wouldn't have been as easy for an individual to buy this much ammunition without drawing attention to himself, but cyber shopping had made everything murkier and transactions much harder to trace. His purchases went to his apartment and were another missed red flag.

BulkAmmo.com advertisements listed a P.O. Box address in St. Louis, but it had no warehouse or office in that city. According to a story in the *St. Louis Dispatch*, BulkAmmo was registered to another company operating under the various names of LuckyGunner.com, Ammoforsale.com, and Ammo.net. All sold ammunition online and had business addresses leading to an "Earth Class Mail" box in different cities, including St. Louis, Atlanta, and Richmond, Virginia. The retailers were owned by a single company, LuckyGunner LLC, with a mailing address in New York City, yet the office address for this firm was in Knoxville, Tennessee. Based on the information contained in its annual report, the company was managed by Jordan Mollenhour and Dustin E. Gross.

Both men had previously worked in real estate and run Mollenhour Homes in a Knoxville subdivision, but when the real estate market collapsed in the 2000s, they transitioned into selling ammunition. Jordan's father, Mike, had once advocated for the repeal of a gun ban in Knoxville's public parks and had begun writing a gun-rights blog, hosted at virtualmilitia.com. In a post written just hours after the Aurora massacre, the older Mullenhour excoriated the culture that allowed "these murderous rampages" and encouraged readers to arm themselves and to start practicing head shots.

LuckyGunner's business address in Knoxville led only to a UPS store in a strip mall. The origins of this ammo cyber-store had come about in late 2008, with the U.S. economy tanking and Barack Obama on the verge of becoming the nation's first African-American president. Conditions were ripe, the people running the company felt, for customers to begin buying ammunition in bulk. The essence of the *St. Louis Dispatch* report was that it had never been easier to get vast quantities of ammo through trails that were very difficult to follow. In July 2012, federal law required no background checks on those buying ammunition and no license to purchase or sell it. There were no limits on how many rounds one could buy and no federal requirement to keep sales records.

Holmes bought 6,300 bullets without raising any warning signs. This ammunition did not come from St. Louis, as one might have assumed by looking at his iPhone after the murders, or from Knoxville, but was shipped from a warehouse in Atlanta. The path from Georgia to Aurora revealed the roots of a booming business. Two months after the Aurora shootings, the U.S. Bureau of Alcohol, Tobacco, Firearms and Explosives granted LuckyGunner a federal license to sell firearms.

■ ■ ■

In early July, Holmes surprisingly reached out to a female grad school classmate. He asked if she'd ever heard of "dysphoric mania," or "mixed mania," which combined manic energy with depression or paranoid delusions.

The woman e-mailed back, wondering if the illness could be managed with treatment.

"It was," he responded vaguely, adding that she should stay away from him, "because I am bad news."

They didn't communicate again.

On July 5, he set up an account on Adultfriendfinder.com, which promotes itself as a place to "find worldwide sex dates, adult matches, hookups, and fuck friends at our popular online sex site."

He posted a personal ad, using the handle "classicjimbo," which included the following question:

"Will you visit me in prison?"

Photographs of Holmes on the site, taken several days before the massacre, show him in the same dyed orange hair that he'd wear to Theater Nine.

According to preliminary hearing testimony, a few hours before midnight on July 20, he put all of his guns and hundreds of rounds of ammunition on the red bedspread in his apartment. He laid out his ballistic helmet, urban assault vest, and groin protector. He slipped dark contact lenses into his eyes and slid a black skull cap down over his curly orange hair, letting out just enough strands to conjure up devilish horns. With his iPhone, he began posing and taking numerous disturbing selfies.

At 11:30 p.m., he left his apartment in his white Hyundai hatchback and drove south toward the Aurora 16 Complex, parking directly behind Theater Nine. Two weeks earlier, he'd used his phone to purchase a ticket for tonight's premiere and to take photos of the theater's interior and specifically the doorjamb on a rear emergency exit near the screen. He'd bought a small piece of blue plastic to clip on the side of this door so that after entering Theater Nine in regular clothing, he could prop the door open with the clip, go back out to his car to load his guns, and change into combat gear. Then he'd re-enter the theater through the cracked rear door.

■ ■ ■

"In the four months between January 2012 and May 2012," says a CU professor, "something jolted Holmes into action, but I believe that this was just when he reached critical mass and decided to go forward. The impulse for doing what he did could have been there years earlier—if not longer."

This view is supported by David Casper and Kafai Suen of Hillcrest Pawnbrokers in San Diego. Holmes had come into their shop in either late 2011 or early 2012 and looked in the firearms section, taking enough time and showing enough interest in the guns to make a lasting impression on both of them.

"Neuroscience labs," says the professor, "can study how people lose their empathy and their feelings for others, but this is very difficult to examine because these things are so hard to measure and quantify. I believe that Holmes's plan to kill was in place long before he failed his exam in June. The reason he failed it is because he was focused much more on his plan than on his studies. It had been in the works for some time. Then something happened."

From a twenty-one-year-old female in school in Boulder, Colorado:

When it happened I was working at a movie theater that was showing the same midnight premiere of The Dark Knight Rises. *We had a nearly full house with five showings and two of them were sold out. At about two a.m. I was watching the movie when we started getting alerted about Aurora. The first reports were that three people were dead. I met with my manager in the lobby to talk about what we should do. The police had already come to our theater and were gathered out front, but we decided to let the movie run until it ended. After that night, we had in-house cops on the premises for the next month.*

At first, I almost didn't believe the news, but then it made sense to me in a way because these movies are such a big deal and the characters have so much influence on young people. People on Facebook started changing their cover photos to reflect the tragedy. My friends keep updated on all these kinds of events. They go behind the headlines and look for more information online or at alternative news sources. We all talked about James Holmes and the victims, but the bigger issue was about us staying connected to each other through social media.

If you don't connect with others in this way or don't have an online presence and feel a part of that world, that can definitely be an issue for people our age. If someone feels he's smarter than everyone else, but isn't connected to his peer group in a meaningful way, you can see how they could get very isolated and act out like that. To me, this connectedness to others is more important than the effect of violent video games or movies on young people. You can really have a presence and a voice now through social media, but if you aren't involved in that world, you might feel very isolated and think that the only impact you can have is by creating a huge disturbance that gets everyone talking about you.

My generation has been tremendously influenced and shaped by new technology and by corporate branding. If you go on a date with a guy and he pulls out an Android phone, you instantly think to yourself, Oh, he's that kind of person. I know this and this and this about him because he has an Android and not an iPhone.

You're very quickly defined by the brands of things you own. Apple and Nike define you. So do other companies and that segregates and separates people in many different ways. These may seem like small things, but there's a lot of pressure on us to be a part of all that. Some people react to it very badly.

People my age are consumed with creating profiles of themselves online. Your Facebook profile defines you as a person, but we tend to confuse this profile with being who we really are. The people I know who do this are actually quite different from their online personalities. They use the technology to make themselves appear something other or something more than what they are. They use it to create fantasies about themselves. They get to escape and to have a different identity. I've fallen into this myself.

XI

Right after the shootings at Theater Nine, the non-wounded survivors were transported to nearby Gateway High School to be interviewed by criminal investigators. This went on for hours until the following morning. Once they were released, a few of them wandered back toward their cars in the large asphalt parking lot located just behind the Century 16 complex, where ten bodies remained inside.

One of the bodies belonged to Alex Sullivan. That weekend, he'd planned on celebrating his twenty-seventh birthday with friends at the midnight showing of *The Dark Knight Rises*. Immediately after the tragedy, Alex's father, Tom, heard reports of the shootings through the media and began calling local hospitals looking for his son, one after the other, frantic for any information. Eight hours after the first 911 calls went out from inside the complex, Tom learned that Alex was still in theater. He'd jumped in front of one of his friends and saved him, sacrificing his own life.

■ ■ ■

At eleven that morning, severe heat bounced off the parking lot like the waves of a slow-growing fire. Everyone assembled here was too busy to pay much attention to the summer of 2012—the hottest on record in Denver—or to notice the thickening exhaust from the white satellite trucks lined up row after row across the pavement. Wires were strewn everywhere, making a crisscross pattern on the asphalt. TV crews from around the country had already arrived in Aurora, less than half a day after the bullets stopped flying. For nearly two decades, these man-made disasters had been erupting throughout the nation with regularity, and the violence was never motivated by anything as commonplace as stealing money or seeking some other tangible, material gain.

The crimes were homegrown terrorism.

By midday Friday, July 20, President Obama announced that he'd visit Aurora the coming Sunday afternoon to meet with local officials and the families of the victims. Christian Bale, one of the stars of *The Dark Knight Rises*, was making plans to travel to Colorado to speak with survivors of the attack. Warner Bros., the studio that had distributed the movie, would contribute $1 million to a local fund. Producer Harvey Weinstein was about to call for a summit of filmmakers to discuss screen violence, but this never came to fruition (he'd make similar efforts in the future, following other mass shootings).

■ ■ ■

Two young men who'd just been released after being debriefed at Gateway High School stared blankly at the reporters jostling to get at them. Their legs were unstill, their hands trembling. They were clearly still in shock but felt the need to speak in public about what they'd witnessed ten hours earlier.

Twenty-year-old Chris Ramos was a barista at a neighborhood Starbucks in Aurora. His shaking fingers held a movie stub from last night's premiere, proving that he was in Theater Nine's fifth row when a gunman burst in through an emergency exit wearing a gas mask and clad all in black. The figure threw what Ramos initially thought were toy bats into the air, part of promoting the movie, but they were canisters of tear gas.

"The first sign that something was wrong," said Ramos, "was when the guy next to me slumped over in his chair. He'd been shot. I crouched down and shielded my seventeen-year-old sister on the floor. I started crying not because I was afraid, but because the tear gas was stinging my eyes."

When the gunman stopped shooting about sixty seconds later, several people around Ramos were dead.

The killer turned and calmly walked toward the rear of the theater "as if nothing had happened."

Media bulletins going out across the United States that morning said that twelve people had been murdered in Aurora and fifty-eight more were wounded in the gunfire, some with paralyzing or crippling injuries that would last for their lifetimes. Twelve other people were wounded trying to escape the theater and would be listed in the final tally of eighty-two victims. But no one talked about Chris Ramos or how the event had affected him. He was collateral damage and would never become part of the statistics surrounding the crime.

Throughout America there were now hundreds or thousands like him who were never checked into the emergency rooms of hospitals, but who'd seen and heard some things they'd never forget.

When a reporter suggested that Ramos take advantage of the psychological counseling being offered to the survivors, he didn't seem to hear. He just kept talking and talking, weaving in front of us in the burning sunlight.

After someone else told him to go home and get some rest, he shook his head and said, "I can't sleep."

■ ■ ■

One person listening to the media bulletins in Denver that morning was a professor at the Anschutz campus who'd had several face-to-face encounters with Holmes during the past school year. He'd listened to his oral presentations and thought the young man had a good future in science.

"I heard about the massacre on the radio as I was driving into work that Friday morning," he says. "When they mentioned the name of the alleged shooter, it didn't mean anything to me. I couldn't put a face to it.

"My first concern was not with the killer, but if I knew anyone who might have been in the Aurora theater last night. After I got to the office, I thought about the name again—James Holmes—and it began to ring a bell. I looked through some photos to see if the name matched the person I remembered. It did, and I could never have imagined him doing this. It's a pretty big step to go from someone who's reclusive and quirky and perhaps a little strange to becoming a mass murderer.

"Before this happened, nobody in our graduate program was concerned with their personal safety. We never talked about it. Now you look out at the students in class and wonder if this one or that one is armed. If we see anyone who seems stressed now, we pay a lot more attention."

From a twenty-six-year-old female in Virginia:

You also have to learn how to deal with pressure. I'm suffocated by everything I'm supposed to do—go to school, get great grades, get a job right away, fit in, and be a huge success.

Follow this one path all the way and you win. Follow another path and you're nobody. The pressure to win is everywhere. It's on top of us pushing down, from grade school on. It feels like you're in a struggle for your survival, even if you have financial resources. My friends and I constantly talk about this. It's a part of our daily reality.

I think there's a reason Adam Lanza went into an elementary school and shot it up and killed all those kids. School is where it all begins.

Interlude

"If you want to understand guys my age," Eric told us again and again when he was nearing twenty, "you have to watch *The Matrix* and *Fight Club*."

For some time we put off viewing the films, but in the end, the movies, once viewed, offered a very revealing window into the young male psyche.

The Matrix is the story of a gifted computer programmer named Neo (a variation on the word *One*). He's trapped inside a simulated reality where humans are controlled by machines that use human bio-electricity as an energy source. The film explores philosophical questions about the nature of reality and evokes "The Cave" allegory put forth by Plato, which asks us to consider whether our experiences are actually real or come out of a world hidden from view.

Neo becomes the one who figures out the system he's trapped inside of and rebels. He escapes the control of the machines and fights against the forces that want to keep him plugged in. Those forces are cleverly represented by Agent Smith, an authority figure who replicates himself all over the movie. There are many Agent Smiths and they're constantly opposing Neo's quest to break free. The only way out is through combat.

In the dramatic climax, Neo, clad in a long black coat, enters a corporate building with guns blazing—an almost exact parallel to the scene that unfolded at Columbine High with Eric Harris and Dylan Klebold three weeks after the film was released in early 1999. The two students were also dressed in dark, floor-length coats and opened fire inside their school.

Neo violently battles the system to win back his humanity. Harris and Klebold unleashed an attack against all of "humanity," as they put it in a recording, unleashing their bloodshed on the carefully selected date of April 20, the 110th birthday of Adolf Hitler. *The Matrix* clearly resonated with a young generation of moviegoers and grossed $460 million worldwide, while winning four Academy Awards. Several other highly successful sequels followed.

Fight Club, which also came out in 1999, takes some of these same themes to another level. The conflict in *The Matrix* is externalized: Neo is combatting real enemies who want to keep him a slave to their mechanized society. In *Fight Club*, Edward Norton plays a nameless, Everyman character with a soft voice, unimposing looks, and a weak personality. A traveling automobile company employee, he's going through life without leaving much of an imprint. He's a good consumer, who's bought all the right Ikea furniture for his home and all the right accessories, and he's moved into a good address, but his life is empty. Something is missing; something is wrong.

He suffers from insomnia and distracts himself from this by attending support groups for people with serious illnesses, expressing his sympathy and fooling others into thinking that he's a victim of their diseases. One disease is testicular cancer, a sly commentary on the male who's become emasculated. (Eric had repeatedly used the term "masculinity in crisis" with us, and these films helped Joyce in particular understand this phrase and why it was important to young men our son's age.) In order to find meaning for himself and a role to play beyond consumerism, Norton's character has taken on the persona of the super-sensitive male.

During a business trip, he meets a rowdy, handsome, and more traditionally masculine-looking man about his age, played by Brad

Pitt. Pitt's character, Tyler Durden, mocks Norton for being so conventional and timid—someone who's just drifting along and passively accepting the world around him. One night they go out for a drink and leaving the bar they get into a fistfight in the parking lot, as other men gather round to watch them. From this event comes the idea of creating a fight club, led by Durden, where men can go and beat each other to a pulp.

"The first rule of fight club," Durden tells the assembled group, "is that you don't talk about fight club."

It's their secret realm, where they can act out their aggression and violence in private, away from women and the rest of society. Durden mentions how many contemporary males have been raised without fathers. Gradually, more and more men are drawn to the club and it becomes a national underground movement. There's something about it they can't resist.

"When the fight was over," the Norton character says, "nothing was solved, but nothing mattered. We all felt saved."

Durden proclaims that his generation of men has no Great War to sacrifice themselves for; they're fighting a *spiritual war* instead.

"Our Great Depression," he tells the fighters, "is our lives . . . We've all been raised on television to believe that one day we'd all be millionaires, and movie gods, and rock stars. But we won't. And we're slowly learning that fact. And we're very, very pissed off."

They must find a cause find worthy of that anger, a cause that makes them feel "special."

With Durden leading the way, the group adopts an anti-corporate, anti-materialistic mindset. He creates "Project Mayhem," whose purpose is to erase all debt in America by destroying the buildings that contain the records of credit card companies. Without this debt, society could start over with a clean slate and be less corrupt and more just—or at least more anarchic.

"If you erase the debt record," the Norton character tells the police, "then we all go back to zero. You'll create total chaos."

The ideas acted out in the movie quickly found some echoes in the outside world. A few weeks after *Fight Club* was released, the "Battle in Seattle" riots broke out in protest of the World Trade Organization's Ministerial Conference and the globalization of the economy. In 2015 in Denver, when a series of well-attended fights broke out near East High School, the police and school officials were quick to quell rumors that they weren't, according to *The Denver Post,* "part of some not-so-underground, organized program, such as in the 1999 movie *Fight Club.*"

The movie's real message went deeper than politics or economics. The hook in the film is that Tyler Durden is not a real person, but a projection of Norton's mind or imagination, his alter ego. Durden/Pitt is the hard-bodied, ideal-looking, irresistible male, as seen in so many underwear ads across the nation. He's the embodiment of the male action hero, male power, and male sex appeal—all the things that Norton finds missing in himself. *He* isn't special, but Durden is.

In the movie, the Brad Pitt character achieves his vision by resorting to minor acts of violence that eventually become much larger. They are all carried out—in his mind—in order to improve society. Male anger, stirred by feelings of impotence or insignificance, is channeled into a kind of social and political activism. If it isn't real activism with an actual political agenda, it is intended to rid the world of evil. And in doing that, you can become a hero.

It is not inaccurate to say that many of the recent young mass shooters have had a passing resemblance to each other and to the Edward Norton character. They've often been pale and frail and not especially handsome (there are exceptions). Their physical appearance caused some of them to be made fun of in school and bullied. Part of their violence has undeniably come from the desire to get even with those who severely hurt their feelings. They decided to take up arms against a world that seemed cruel.

Unlike *The Matrix, Fight Club* originally flopped at the box office. It's a more subtle and thought-provoking movie, and it took time for the story to sink in and to find an audience. Over the years since its release, it's become one of 20th Century Fox's biggest-selling home media products.

■ ■ ■

Fight Club, a movie about male insecurity and perceived male inadequacy and how this can lead one into despair and even violence, has a profundity for men that it likely doesn't have for women—some of whom have found it to be puerile—and that profundity is still there when you watch the film at age forty or fifty or sixty. Norton initially tries to be highly sensitive, but then embraces his other side—the violent stud who gets the leading woman in the movie, Helena Bonham Carter. As Pitt and Carter make wild love in the bedroom, Norton can only stand in another room and listen to them. Pretty much everything that men deal with in their most private realms is captured in the film.

Fight Club conveys the message that the way to have a real impact on society is to do something huge and bloody. And in some ways, it's a very difficult message to counter. The movie stars who embody this core message naturally become onscreen heroes and role models. They are the people who make a difference, and they are trying—they tell themselves—to build a better world. The truth is that all men have a little Tyler Durden inside of them and try to come to grips with it, for better or worse. Finding the balance between the action-oriented Pitt character and the thoughtful Norton character is a struggle that men rarely talk about, but it never goes away.

The movie brilliantly dramatizes this inner battle and shows viewers precisely where men are vulnerable. Without father figures or other healthy male role models to provide some guidance through this emotional maze, men can end up filled with resentment, rage, self-judgment, and pain at not being "special" in any way at all.

■ ■ ■

"A lot of males of my generation," Eric told us more than once when discussing these movies, "have been raised without dads. They try to act as if this doesn't bother or affect them, but it does. They're insecure about it, but never really talk about that. They don't have male role models who can show them how to behave not just physically, but emotionally. Or their fathers are so caught up in their work that they never take the time to do this. How do you deal with anger or fear when it comes up inside of you? How do you manage yourself when something really upsets or hurts you? If you don't have a parent, especially of your own gender, to look to for this kind of guidance, it makes it doubly hard to grow up."

As Eric became an adolescent, Steve often told him that no matter what happened with him the future, he could tell his father about it. That meant anything, anything at all, about sex or girls or problems at school or trouble with other kids or money or personal issues that are very hard to speak about or anything else that he was willing to bring up. There were no boundaries on what could be communicated, if Eric felt the need to open up, or if he was in a situation and was afraid to tell us about it. Steve had not grown up feeling that he could do this with his own father; he'd wanted to protect his parents from his inner life and from some parts of his external life, and he wasn't able to confide in his dad until they were both much older.

This is not to suggest that Steve and Eric talked all the time. They didn't. In fact, throughout middle school and high school, there were long periods when Eric wasn't at all communicative, but the offer was always on the table.

■   ■   ■

After viewing the movies, we both came to the same conclusion: our son had pointed us in a direction worth exploring, and we were beginning to see the mass-shooting phenomenon from a broader and more cultural perspective.

"Tyler Durden as the super male," Eric said, "is what *Fight Club* is all about. Many of these school shooters, like the Edward Norton character, feel ineffectual. Every aspect of their world has told them that they're not special, not good enough. Our society says that not everyone can win. So much of what young men deal with now has to do with advertising. You don't have the right life until you have this job, this car, this wife, this house, and everything else that's perfect. You're inadequate until you have all of these things. And young men my age don't feel they can ever achieve all that. They experience this as pressure and they're angry about it. The pressure isn't getting any better, in terms of being relieved. It's getting worse.

"The kids who commit these crimes aren't justified in what they do, but this is one of the sources of their feelings. Everyone my age has watched *Fight Club* and it's a satire about how men try to resist this internal pressure. Advertising doesn't allow you to feel happy or be satisfied with what you are. You work at a job that you don't like to buy what you don't need. How do you not feel lonely and isolated in those circumstances? How do you not feel alienated from the culture? How do you start to feel that you can have some effect that's positive?

"The movie is about men feeling emasculated because they don't look like the images in Calvin Klein ads. Believe me, this is a big deal to guys, not just to young women. You have no idea. The mass shooters are not alpha males. Young dudes want to feel empowered and the only way some of them can do it is by joining the military, where they'll man you up. Or you can be in the fake military and play violent video games like *Call of Duty,* which re-create all of America's recent wars. If you're weak in the real world, in that realm you can kill people much bigger than you and feel good about yourself for a *while.*"

THE SPIRAL NOTEBOOK

XII

On Monday morning, July 23, as Holmes came to court for his initial appearance before Judge William Sylvester, a bomb squad kept working to disarm the IEDs in his apartment, as they'd been doing for the past three days. While the legal proceedings got underway, a FedEx package showed up at the Anschutz campus central administration building. A classic Art Deco structure with an elegant façade and a marble interior, it was a holdover from when this address had been home to Fitzsimmons Army Base. It was the building that held the office of Dr. Lynne Fenton.

After being taken into custody on Friday, Holmes quickly told the police about the IEDs in his apartment. But there was some information he hadn't shared with them. Over that weekend, he'd confessed to one of his lawyers that hours before the shootings, he'd mailed a package to Dr. Fenton at the Anschutz campus; it could be easily identified because of how boldly he'd written his return address across the front. The lawyer phoned the CU medical school to let them know about the package and that it was absolutely a private communication between a patient and his psychiatrist. Therefore, went his legal argument, it could never be used as evidence against Holmes. His defense team wanted it returned to them as soon as possible.

That Sunday evening, Doug Abraham, Chief of the CU Police Department, was contacted by Dr. Robert Feinstein, Chairman of Outpatient

Services for the CU hospital, who was also Dr. Fenton's supervisor. Dr. Feinstein had received a call from a Holmes representative who said that the suspect wanted the package back—unopened. Chief Abraham passed this request along to Police Commander Steve Smith.

Early on Monday morning, the CU police conducted a search of Dr. Fenton's office and found a FedEx package slid under her door. It instantly raised suspicions, but because Holmes's address wasn't written on it, the package was deemed irrelevant to the investigation.

Several hours later, Chief Abraham learned of another heavily stamped white envelope, which had just come into the loading dock of the campus mailroom. It showed Holmes's address, so they cleared the building of about fifty employees and cordoned off the perimeter around the dock. The authorities called in the Adams County bomb squad, which soon arrived at the scene with a five-ton truck and a robot. The FBI was sending in a weapons-of-mass-destruction expert to be joined by environmental safety personnel and members of the Aurora Police Department.

All of this was just one front of an investigation now expanding outward across the United States, which would eventually include 444 police officers and fifty-six lab personnel. The case would generate more than 40,000 pages of discovery and 3,500 potential witnesses. Forensic experts who searched Holmes's Internet browsing history on the PC in his apartment would find, among many other things, a website called "Rational Insanity." As many would speculate after the massacre, Holmes was studying himself in his classes and apparently looking online for insight into his own mental condition. Or he may have been gathering information for an insanity defense in the future. Whatever his motive, he was looking into some very sophisticated psychological concepts leading up to the shootings.

At the campus mailroom that Monday morning, the robot was activated to pick up the package Holmes had sent to Dr. Fenton and place it inside a hooded container. Sensors were attached to the container, and the envelope was x-rayed for bio-chemical hazards and explosives. The reading came up zero. Wearing a gas mask and a crinkled plastic head covering, a technician then carefully removed the package's contents, pulling out a brown spiral notebook, decorated with Holmes's name and an infinity symbol. The title on the notebook read, "Of Life."

The officers at the mailroom studied the notebook, and at least two of them, Aurora Police Detective Alton Reed and Chief Abraham, handled it during the course of the day, the Chief poking it with a pen. As Reed rifled through the pages wearing latex gloves, some burnt $20 bills tumbled out. Reed would later testify at a pre-trial hearing that he'd only thumbed through the notebook to see if there were any more bills inside. He claimed that he hadn't scrutinized any of the pages or read any of Holmes's drawings and writings.

"I just kind of fanned through it," he said.

For his part, Chief Abraham admitted that by handling the notebook, he'd been "careless."

Reed, Abraham, and all the other official personnel overseeing the package that day denied that they'd perused the notebook's contents or spoken about them with anyone in the media.

Based on their statements in court, none of them grasped the significance of the burnt money. In *The Dark Knight*, The Joker had set fire to a huge stack of American currency worth around $30 million in order to make a social/political statement: Money was corrupting, and society could easily be controlled or manipulated by its hunger for financial gain.

Most of Monday, July 23, was devoted to the robotic testing and the human examination of the envelope and the notebook. Around ten p.m. that night, Sergeant Matthew Fyles of the Aurora Police Department came to the mailroom with a search warrant and took the notebook into custody. Like the police before them, prosecutors would contend that these pages were clearly relevant to the investigation and part of the evidence against Holmes, and that they should be allowed to view its contents.

From a twenty-six-year-old male working in the entertainment business on the West Coast:

> In these huge mass shooting cases, we see very clearly the individual crimes, but we don't see how deeply the overall community is now divided against itself. It's the whole society that's in conflict with itself and that conflict plays out within the media and our politics and the legal system too. That's why it's so hard to find out the things about James Holmes that we really need to know. Everyone involved in the case just wants to cover his own ass so the public doesn't learn what's important. Instead of being able to discover who this person was and how he ended up where he is we fight over the right to have access to anything of value.
>
> We have the right to know who James Holmes is and why he did these things. We have the right to know what happened to him before he became a killer. That's a small thing to expect when a dozen people are dead and a lot more have been wounded.

XIII

As news of the spiral notebook leaked out, Jana Winter, a Fox-TV reporter from New York, broadcast via the Internet that the spiral notebook was "full of details about how he was going to kill people" and contained "drawings and illustrations of the massacre." Some were already calling it the Rosetta Stone of the case. Winter cited unnamed law-enforcement sources as having offered up this information. If it were true, and if these details had indeed come from law enforcement, it was a clear violation of a July 23 gag order Judge Sylvester had imposed on everyone involved in the investigation and the ongoing courtroom proceedings.

The gag order, combined with an almost total lack of information coming from the schools Holmes had attended, his family, and virtually everyone he'd ever known, all but closed down the story of his background and his academic, medical, and psychiatric history. It made him an invisible man—while being the most-talked-about mass killer in America. Right after the shootings, the University of Colorado advised its staff to get rid of all 3,800 of Holmes's CU e-mails, but soon gave up this mission because it was basically impossible to accomplish.

Despite the gag order, media outlets began requesting everything from the university e-mails related to Holmes. Attorney Steven Zansberg, who represented numerous press organizations, spoke to *The*

Denver Post about the stance taken by CU: "No doubt they're capable of protecting student privacy, medical privacy—that's what they have to do, [but] they don't just get to come in here and say please spare us that hassle."

CU spokeswoman Jacque Montgomery issued a statement saying that "these legal processes will ultimately present the full history of James Holmes's interactions with the University of Colorado, its educators, and its medical providers."

At the time, that seemed like a reasonable position, but neither Montgomery nor anyone else could have predicted where the case was headed or how interminably long it would take to get there. More than two years after she delivered this pronouncement, none of this critical history had been presented to anyone but two judges, a handful of lawyers, and less than a handful of psychiatrists.

Instead of learning more about Holmes's educational and emotional journey through the school system, all doorways were sealed off. What had happened in grade school that had caused some people to see him as a bully, yet others to hint that he'd been bullied himself? What had gone on inside his household as a child, when his parents were confronted with a highly imaginative boy given to flights of fancy? What had created his intense sense of isolation that had only deepened with age? What had he done at UC-Riverside that had pushed him in the direction of taking LSD and tampering with a mind growing increasingly fragile? What had nudged him, after moving to Aurora, to enter into a comic-book world and to act out his violent fantasies?

The best available clues to all these mysteries were contained in the pages of the spiral notebook, but almost no one had access to it. Because Holmes had been a standout PhD candidate in a field that focused on the brain and mental illness, it's possible that his writings could have provided some insight into his descent into bloodshed—insight that educators, parents, media, law enforcement, and others throughout America were more than eager to have. But it remained off-limits to all of those groups.

■ ■ ■

Jana Winter's controversial report on the notebook intensified the tug-of-war over its contents. Within days of the shooting, a battle was underway between the Arapahoe County District Attorney's Office, set to prosecute the case, and the Colorado Public Defender lawyers, representing Holmes. A fundamental legal question was in play. Did the notebook contain privileged, confidential material because of the relationship between Holmes and his former therapist, Dr. Lynne Fenton? Colorado law protected "any information acquired in attending the patient that was necessary to enable him or her to prescribe or act for the patient." Or had this confidentiality shield been waived because their therapy sessions had ended six weeks before the crime? When does a patient's relationship with a doctor officially end? Does hearing threats from a patient trump confidentiality? All of this was unexplored legal territory and could become precedent-setting aspects of the case as it unfolded.

Prosecutors contended that when Holmes had stopped seeing Dr. Fenton on June 11, he and the psychiatrist no longer had a professional relationship, a confidential relationship, or a relationship of any kind. The notebook could then be used as evidence to try to establish, as they saw it, Holmes's longstanding and deeply premeditated homicidal intentions. Those intentions and his elaborate plans for the massacre clearly made him sane at the time of the crime. He should stand trial, like any other defendant, for at least a dozen counts of first-degree murder.

Wrong, the defense argued.

On July 20, Holmes and Dr. Fenton still had an ongoing, confidential patient-doctor relationship. No information between them could *ever* become public or part of a criminal prosecution. The lines were drawn and the notebook was at the heart of the conflict.

At a very early and very heated three-and-a-half-hour hearing on the case in late August 2012, Holmes's counsel went even further in attempting to demonstrate that he still had a patient-doctor relationship with Lynne Fenton. One of his lawyers, Tamara Brady, told the judge that at 12:31 a.m. on July 20, the defendant had used his iPhone to dial the number for CU Health Services. Students were given this number in case they needed emergency medical or psychiatric help.

Less than ten minutes before the attack, Brady theorized, Holmes may have reached out to Dr. Fenton because the CU Health Services switchboard had the ability to connect him with her.

The University of Colorado Hospital marketing director Brad Fixler did acknowledge that the switchboard had received a call at 12:31 a.m., but that was all he conceded.

"Can I help you?" the operator had responded.

For a full seven seconds, the line was silent, the caller either unable or unwilling to speak.

Then the person hung up.

During the hearing, Judge Sylvester ruled that the spiral notebook was unavailable to the prosecutors because they couldn't prove that the doctor-patient relationship between Holmes and Fenton had ended. The prosecution resisted this legal interpretation, but all of the lawyers were working in a gray area because a mass shooter had never done anything like this before going on a rampage. Prosecutor Karen Pearson challenged the judge's position, finding it illogical: Holmes wasn't going to be in any future therapy sessions with Dr. Fenton, she said, because he "intended to be dead or in prison after this shooting."

Tamara Brady, who normally had a soft voice that tended to shake in the courtroom, quickly overcame that tendency. She fiercely objected to Pearson's argument and accused the prosecutor of making "many gigantic leaps" in her thinking to reach this conclusion about Holmes and his therapist. She reiterated that a doctor-patient relationship still existed between the two even if Dr. Fenton hadn't seen the defendant since June 11.

Dr. Fenton herself made her only courtroom appearance at this hearing (following the shootings, she'd received so much attention and so many threats that she'd gone into hiding). She testified that she believed that her relationship with Holmes had ended with his final appointment. In her view no professional connection between them existed on the afternoon of July 19, when he'd mailed her the package.

By sending her the notebook, Fenton told the judge, he was saying, "I'm feeling bad. Please stop me. Do something. Help me."

In an aggressive maneuver that would characterize the defense from the very beginning, Holmes's legal team insisted that their client's actions with both the notebook and the phone call at 12:31 a.m. showed that he *knew* he was mentally ill and needed Dr. Fenton's assistance. Under these conditions, the spiral notebook had to be protected by patient-doctor confidentiality throughout the duration of any legal proceedings—unless Holmes eventually decided to plead not guilty by reason of insanity. At that point, under the rules of discovery, the defendant would waive the right to confidentiality and be compelled to turn over the notebook and other materials relating to his mental state at the time of the crime. Thus far, the defense had not revealed its strategy.

■ ■ ■

Other possible explanations for Holmes's behavior did not surface in court that afternoon. Had he sent the notebook and made the midnight call as part of his overall strategy? Were they just two more pieces of an enormously complex scheme he'd thought up, planned out, and then executed in the months leading up to the shootings—all done to make him appear insane after the massacre? Was he already plotting his legal defense long before he'd armed himself and driven to the theater?

Was he genuinely crazy, a true madman who actually thought he was The Joker? Or was he highly calculating and "crazy like a fox," the phrase that the public and reporters kept asking themselves each time they gathered at the Arapahoe County Justice Center for Holmes's next courtroom appearance? Or was he a high-functioning schizophrenic, like Ted Kaczynski, the Unabomber?

One other interpretation for his actions existed, but it wasn't much discussed. Had Holmes believed that he, like so many mass killers before him, would die at the theater as soon as the police arrived? Had he mailed in the notebook a few hours before driving to the movie complex to explain to Dr. Fenton and perhaps the world why he'd done what he had, once his life was over?

The best way to answer all of those questions was through a full and public examination of the notebook itself. When it was discovered a few days after the massacre, that possibility seemed not just likely, but imminent. If Jana Winter could get law enforcement personnel to talk about what they'd seen in these pages, surely the rest of us would soon get the same chance. Before long, even the prosecutors came to this conclusion and gave up their fight to gain access to the notebook. They believed that Holmes was about to plead not guilty by reason of insanity and the defense would then, by law, be forced to turn this piece of evidence over to them.

With that in mind, prosecutor Rich Orman told the judge, "There's a high degree of likelihood that whatever privilege exists in the notebook will end up being waived by the defendant."

But Orman could not have predicted how entangled things would become or how difficult it would be for anyone to see these pages.

From a twenty-four-year-old female in Denver:

> *When these massacres happen, people always ask, "Why didn't the shooter just kill himself and leave everyone else alone?" Because when you feel like a victim, you want to get even with the world. You want to make sense of something that is senseless.*

XIV

The bomb squad that had worked for days to defuse Holmes's booby-trapped apartment had found numerous medications in his home, including sedatives, ibuprofen, and Sertraline, the generic version of the antidepressant Zoloft. It was unclear where the drugs had come from or if they'd been prescribed to him. Brought to market in 1991 by Pfizer, Sertraline was usually prescribed for major depressive disorder in adults or for panic attacks, anxiety disorders, and obsessive-compulsive behavior in adults and children. By the time Holmes was taking the drug, Sertraline had become the third-most popular antidepressant in America, with more than 37,000,000 prescriptions. The bomb squad also found the anti-anxiety drug Clonazepam, which treats panic disorder and which Roche markets in the United States under the name Klonopin. In 1975, Klonopin was originally brought to market as a medication for epileptic seizures. Known as a "benzodiazepine drug," it has sedative, anticonvulsant, and hypnotic properties.

The Internet is filled with stories about people's experience of going sideways on these "benzos."

In November 2014, writer Diana Spechler published an article in *Salon* about her time on Klonopin: "Well-known benzo side effects include 'emotional clouding' and 'loss of creativity' . . . 'I have not been able to feel anything . . . in three years. I can't even cry right,' wrote one member of BenzoBuddies Community Forum, an online group for people withdrawing from benzodiazepines."

In 1986, a psychiatrist prescribed Klonopin to Fleetwood Mac singer Stevie Nicks following her withdrawal from cocaine addiction. The drug, she later told *US Weekly*, "turned me into a zombie," and her rehab from Klonopin felt as if "somebody opened up a door and pushed me into hell." A decade later, actress Margaux Hemingway killed herself after overdosing on a barbiturate-benzodiazepine mixture, and Hollywood producer Don Simpson accidentally did the same. A decade after that, Klonopin was found in the body of Anna Nicole Smith, and when a physician prescribed Klonopin to author David Foster Wallace, who was suffering from depression, he went into his backyard and hung himself.

In 2013, the Pulitzer Prize–winning investigative website, ProPublica, published "Dollars for Docs," an article about the financial compensation drug companies provide to physicians. It revealed a database of more than 17,000 doctors who received "speaker fees" and other funds from eight drug companies in 2009–10, with compensation totaling $320 million. The major pharmaceutical companies have recently devoted more resources to lobbying than any other American industry, spending $227,808,563 in 2014. By comparison, the oil and gas business spent $140,389,740 and commercial banks only $60,427,384.

■ ■ ■

"A lot of doctors," says a neuroscientist at Anschutz, "don't really know much about how all these drugs work. They just look for the effects on the patients that they feel are beneficial. It's very difficult to get the right mixture of drugs—if you're taking both anti-anxiety medication and antidepressants. As a physician, you experiment until you think you've gotten it right. You look for the optimum concentration of each drug, but we don't yet know enough to say precisely that this is the best drug or best combination of drugs for a specific patient."

Says another member of the Anschutz campus faculty, "I believe that we currently understand only about 1 percent of how the brain actually works. We don't know how vast parts of it function and we know almost nothing about the intricacies of the frontal lobe. Every society likes to compare the brain to the most advanced technological device that it's been able to come up with. For the ancient Romans, it was the aqueduct. For us, it's obviously the computer, but this really isn't a very accurate comparison.

"Imagine a circuit board. It's fixed in your computer and it doesn't change. With the brain, if you think about something, the neuronal connections get stronger or weaker based on what you're thinking about or on how much you're thinking about it. Sometimes, the connections between the neurons can get broken. A nerve cell has all these processes going on and it might be connected to ten thousand other cells and these connections can be excitatory or inhibitory.

"Every single one of these cells can get stronger or weaker, based on the experience of the individual, and each cell can also change how it responds to other cells. The brain is far more complex than anything we've ever built. If you take illegal drugs or play video games two or three hours a day, you can strengthen your aggressive impulses and weaken your empathetic ones. If you become obsessed with something, that impulse gets reinforced in the brain. If you start to think that fantasy is reality, this also gets reinforced. All this would have more effect on someone who's already psychologically abnormal.

"I study the brain for a living and I can tell you one thing: playing around with any of these drugs is dangerous."

■ ■ ■

In April 2013, Ted Gup, a fellow of the Edmond J. Safra Center for Ethics at Harvard University, wrote an impassioned editorial for the *The New York Times* entitled "Diagnosis: Human." He pointed out that 11 percent of American school-age children, or 6.4 million kids, have received a diagnosis of attention deficit hyperactivity disorder. His own "rambunctious" son, David, had been diagnosed with this as a small child, and a psychiatrist had prescribed medication for the youngster, even before meeting him.

Gup resisted the diagnosis . . . for a while. After hesitating for a year, he finally bought Ritalin for David and then Adderall.

When David was a college senior, he was found dead from a fatal mixture of alcohol and heroin, which left his father haunted by a "system that devalues talking therapy and rushes to medicate, inadvertently sending a message that self-medication, too, is perfectly acceptable."

In May 2013, the American Psychiatric Association published its *D.S.M. 5*: the *Diagnostic and Statistical Manual of Mental Disorders*. Surprising certain elements in the psychiatric community, the APA included depression to encompass some forms of grief, because of the symptoms of loss of interest in life, loss of appetite, irregular sleep patterns, and low functionality.

"Ours is an age," Gup wrote, "in which the airwaves and media are one large drug emporium that claims to fix everything from sleep to sex. I fear that being human is itself fast becoming a condition. It's as if we are trying to contain grief, and the absolute pain of a loss like mine."

In Gup's view, Americans had become more and more disassociated and estranged from normal parts of both life and death. The society was increasingly uncomfortable with all kinds of difficulties, including the pain that came with aging and mortality.

"Challenge and hardship have become pathologized and monetized," he wrote. "Instead of enhancing our coping skills, we undermine them and seek shortcuts where there are none, eroding the resilience upon which each of us, at some point in our lives, must rely."

By looking at grief as a symptom of depression, Gup contended, it helped undermine the very qualities and experiences that make us human: our love and emotional connections to each other.

"A broken heart," he wrote, "is not a medical condition, and . . .

medication is ill-suited to repair some tears. Time does not heal all wounds, closure is a fiction, and so too is the notion that God never asks of us more than we can bear. Enduring the unbearable is sometimes exactly what life asks of us."

■ ■ ■

Dr. Jeffrey Gold is a Denver-based mental health clinical pharmacy specialist/psycho-pharmacologist. He too is critical of the over-medication of the American population.

"Giving Adderall and Ritalin now to all these young people and diagnosing them with ADD [attention deficit disorder]," he says, "is just another aspect of our country's massive reliance on drugs. This is a function of how clinicians are being trained and of how much they're influenced by Big Pharma [the major drug companies] to diagnosis and prescribe these drugs. Many clinicians get money from the drug companies to do this . . . You have to be a skeptical consumer of these substances."

According to a study at Northwestern University, the number of children and young people diagnosed with attention deficit hyperactivity disorder (ADHD) shot up 66 percent between 2000 and 2010.

"It's hard for me," says Dr. Gold, "to just accept this so-called ADD 'epidemic' that people now talk about. It comes from the whole mindset of, 'I don't feel good, so I deserve a drug.' Some kids in class might not be paying perfect attention because different children learn differently. They might need more time with a teacher than they're getting, instead of being given a drug. The message is that if you don't fall into line with the system, we'll give you a drug, rather than addressing how to confront learning problems and how to cope better."

According to the Substance Abuse and Mental Health Services Administration of the Department of Health and Human Services, the number of eighteen- to thirty-four-year-olds who've ended up in emergency rooms after taking Adderall, Ritalin, or similar drugs had quadrupled in slightly more than half a decade. In 2005, there were 5,600 of these visits. In 2011, they reached 23,000 and were highest among eighteen- to twenty-five-year-olds. More than half of the patients admitted to the hospital staff that they'd gotten the drugs from a friend or a relative, at no charge.

The drugs were often taken in combination with alcohol, which hid the effects of being drunk and could easily escalate the risk of alcohol poisoning and alcohol-related injuries.

"Zoloft," says Dr. Gold of one of the drugs Holmes was taking, "is an anti-depressant with a primary indication for depression from PTSD. Withdrawing from it can be severe. It can be like having horrific anxiety to the point of trying to crawl out of your skin. Antidepressants bring up your lows and take down your highs. You don't feel the same range of emotions when you're on them. I absolutely feel that some of these drugs, like antidepressants, are being overprescribed."

Klonopin, Dr. Gold said of another substance Holmes was on, "is an anti-anxiety drug. It's addictive and particularly concerning. There's no dosage ceiling on how much you can take. It's like an opiate—you can keep taking more and more. There are longterm consequences from doing this and withdrawing from it can be very bad. It can decrease your cognitive functions and bring on significant medical problems, like seizures. You can even die from it. This is what happened to Heath Ledger. He was taking a combination of these drugs and he took a little too much of too many of them and it killed him.

"Taking a hallucinogenic with these other drugs can very easily put people into extreme mental states and you can't even guess at the outcomes. We've seen a number of these mass shootings from young white men of privilege who feel that things should always go their way, because that's what they're used to in life. When things don't go their way, or when they feel powerless and ineffective, some of them simply can't deal with it."

Echoing Ted Gup, Dr. Gold advocates teaching people better coping skills, as opposed to avoiding reality through drugs.

"Mixing beer or other forms of alcohol," he says, "with a drug cocktail that contains Klonopin can be very risky. Klonopin is like beer in a pill, but it's much, much stronger. Two drinks on Klonopin are like having eight drinks without it. It can be a real disinhibitor."

Inside Holmes's apartment, the bomb squad found fifty empty beer bottles and another notebook containing a drawing of a game featuring a maze with a serial killer. They found a backpack with an unsigned withdrawal form from the University of Colorado Anschutz Medical Campus. They also found a shooting target stand, a note from Holmes's mother about insurance, and a calendar with only one day marked on it: July 20, 2012.

From the twenty-six-year-old male in south Texas:

> *People my age are using antidepressants and anti-anxiety drugs and sleeping pills—anything they can get their hands on. Most do it for entertainment purposes like when they go to a concert or camping. The drugs you "roll on" are really popular now and the main one is Ecstasy and its derivatives. One is Molly and taking it has nothing to do with feeling one with the universe or having a spiritual experience or exploring your consciousness. It's for total entertainment value because it makes everything feel like sex.*

XV

In Holmes's apartment, the bomb squad found a trip wire leading from the front door to a thermos filled with glycerine. The thermos tilted over a frying pan full of potassium permanganate. If these two chemicals were combined, they'd create a spark, causing a chain reaction that would produce flames, igniting the other nearby explosives. A remote-controlled pyrotechnic box sat atop the refrigerator and was filled with six-inch firework shells. Because The Joker had bombed a hospital in *The Dark Knight*, Holmes had intended to level the building where he and other CU medical students now lived.

According to FBI bomb technician Garrett Gumbinner, a remote-control device, in addition to the trip wire placed on his apartment's front door, had been placed outside the building in a trash bag, along with a toy car and a boom box connected to a timer. When he left for the theater around 11:30 p.m. on July 19, Holmes thought that if no one triggered the interior wire, someone passing by on the sidewalk would reach into the bag, pick up the car, touch the remote, and set off the bombs. To heighten the destruction, he'd soaked his carpets with oil and gasoline. Gumbinner would later testify that during or after the massacre Holmes hoped that "someone would call the police and that the police would respond to his apartment . . . in order to divert police resources" away from Century 16.

Scattered around the apartment were an online receipt for a ticket to *The Dark Knight Rises* and a Batman mask, along with ten gallons of gasoline, thirty homemade hand grenades, motor oil, ignition systems, and paper shooting targets. A black box with a red blinking light held dozens of softball-shaped firework shells full of explosive powder. On the walls were posters for the movie *Pulp Fiction* and the paintball series *Soldiers of Misfortune*.

Holmes owned several action video games, including the role-playing *Oblivion* and the futuristic military strategy game *StarCraft*. Set in the twenty-fifth century, *StarCraft* involves three species—humans, insectoid aliens, and humanoids—all fighting for dominance in deep space. Many consider it one of the best and most important games ever with sales far in excess of ten million worldwide (the top players around the globe compete in televised tournaments). A third video game retrieved from Holmes's residence was the role-playing *Skyrim*, among the most popular for males sixteen to twenty-five. The game revolved around the player's efforts to conquer Alduin, a Dragon out to destroy the world. In the first week of its 2011 release, *Skyrim* shipped seven million copies to retailers.

It took nearly four days for the bomb squad to dismantle all the explosives enough for them to be transported to a field outside Denver, where they were safely detonated. On the day of the massacre, Aurora police Lieutenant Thomas Wilkes, the incident commander at Holmes's apartment, had felt that this "building would go" and their primary mission now was to the "defend the other buildings around it." In part because of Holmes's lucidity and willingness to speak with detectives that afternoon about defusing his elaborate explosive designs, another catastrophe was averted. Given the full range of possibilities for mayhem that he'd envisioned, the aftermath of the shootings was handled about as well as anyone could have expected.

■ ■ ■

"We've done a very good job of learning how to react to these tragedies once they've occurred," says Denver therapist Joycee Kennedy, a first responder at the shootings at Columbine High. The author of *Bridging Worlds: Understanding and Facilitating Adolescent Recovery from the Trauma of Abuse,* Kennedy was also contacted after the Aurora killings. "We've developed excellent means for helping victims with psychological first aid, but we're failing badly at preventing these mass murders from erupting. I feel very, very sorry for Dr. Fenton and for what lies ahead for her, but I'm also very disappointed in the mental health system, especially after what took place right here at Columbine.

"In these circumstances, it's standard operating procedure to put a James Holmes into the seventy-two-hour psychiatric evaluation program, but they didn't do that. People like Holmes are very smart, so no one wants to believe that a merit scholar with a federal grant can be a mass murderer, but his intelligence is only part of the story. In school, he was probably studying himself and how his own mind functioned, but he was very detached from his emotional impact on the world.

"Then came the multiple stressors leading up to the shootings—he messed up an oral exam and dropped out of school. His lifelong goal had just evaporated. He had no income to pay the rent. In Denver, he'd built up no friendships and no social structure to fall back on.

"For anyone to turn this violent, his emotional-sensory system had to be impaired or completely shut down. He could no longer feel other people. When your emotional-sensory system is working, you cry in front of a therapist, you get sick to your stomach, you feel bad about your thoughts, and you show what you're feeling physically. Things happen that a therapist can observe. We have ways of measuring these physical reactions and an in-depth evaluation would have revealed all this.

"If Holmes enters an insanity plea in court, it's completely meaningless. He was highly deliberate in planning the attack and indifferent to the consequences. He should plead guilty to the charges, but he probably won't and the university will try to seal his records, including his therapeutic ones, because they're terrified of the liability issues. This is all wrong because it keeps us from learning what we need to know about these events."

In the spring of 2014, almost two years after the massacre, this fear of liability—along with the death threats that had come to Dr. Fenton—caused mental health providers and state lawmakers to take action. Working together, they drafted House Bill 1271, passed unanimously by the Colorado House and Senate. The bill would permit mental health providers to report on threats against locations and on threats against specific groups or individuals, while offering them immunity from potential civil lawsuits.

■ ■ ■

"I've met and worked with Dr. Fenton," says psycho-pharmacologist Dr. Jeffrey Gold, "and I think she's a very good and well-respected doctor. No one could have predicted what Holmes was going to do. I feel very bad for her because psychiatrists don't have a crystal ball. In my mind, this isn't a case about her not diagnosing schizophrenia or latent schizophrenia in her patient. I say that because of all the planning and strategy that went into the shootings. It was very well thought out and put together. To me, it feels more like a bitter message being sent to society by someone who wanted to be a super-villain and then became one."

"Mass shootings," says Joycee Kennedy, "aren't about intelligence or brain structures or genetics, but emotional numbness. We're seeing this everywhere now in our society and we're watching it explode into violence again and again. The rising stars in the psychiatric or neuroscience field look at brain patterns or neurotransmissions far more than at emotions. They're missing the boat and the emotional clues that are there before these things happen. If James Holmes had been my patient, I'd never practice therapy again. My sense of guilt would be too overwhelming."

Seven million Americans currently suffer from mental illness, and half are untreated.

"We don't have a criminal justice problem in this country," Kennedy says. "We have a mental health crisis because the at-risk population isn't getting the psychiatric care it needs. It's all part of the larger health care issues we need to look at now. These events are there to make us focus on what we've been avoiding.

"The Aurora murders represent a huge opportunity to educate the public about the effects of emotional numbness and about how the psychiatric community isn't paying enough attention to this condition. It's imperative that we finally learn something from this tragedy."

From a twenty-nine-year-old female working in the educational field in New Mexico:

> We're all starting to feel less safe and more vulnerable. I get nervous going to a mall or sitting in a room with other people. I look at them more closely now. I check where the exits are. You can now kill fifty people in about thirty seconds, if you have the right weapons.

XVI

One in four American adults—roughly fifty-seven million people—experiences a mental health disorder every year, yet less than a third receive treatment. In 2000, a *New York Times* investigation looked at one hundred shooting rampages and found that at least half of the killers had signs of serious mental health problems. In 2001, Harvard Professor Ronald Kessler reported that most Americans with mental health disorders don't seek help because of our national belief in "rugged individualism"—people want to "to solve the problem on their own." For young adults, the reality is even more challenging. The National Institutes of Medical Health estimates that 8 percent of eighteen- to twenty-four-year-olds have a serious mental illness. Some experts have concluded that their best chance of getting adequate treatment comes from being arrested and incarcerated.

The issue of criminal insanity would emerge as the core question in the case of James Holmes. The Colorado "Insanity Law" reads:

1. The applicable test of insanity shall be, and the jury shall be so instructed: "A person who is so diseased or defective in mind at the time of the commission of the act as to be incapable of distinguishing right from wrong with respect to that act is not accountable. But care should be taken not to confuse such mental

disease or defect with moral obliquity, mental depravity, or passion growing out of anger, revenge, hatred, or other motives, and
kindred evil conditions, for when the act is induced by any of
these causes the person is accountable to the law."

2. The term "diseased or defective in mind," as used in subsection
(1) of this section, does not refer to an abnormality manifested
only by repeated criminal or otherwise antisocial conduct."

In Colorado, the state has the burden of proving that a defendant is
sane. (In numerous other states, the burden is on the defense to prove
that the accused is insane.) Also in Colorado, a defendant could ask
for a mental health evaluation, and those examining him would be
chosen by officials at the Colorado Mental Health Institute at Pueblo.
Prosecutors did not have the right to select their own mental health
examiners for a defendant, a sore spot in many DAs' offices around the
state—which would become even more so as Holmes's case unfolded.

Says Denver neurologist Mark Spitz, who's treated many patients
with varying degrees of mental illness: "Holmes was probably using
the grad school experience to look at himself and his own mind and
mental health disorders. Schizophrenia becomes much more evident
in some people in their twenties. It can intensify as you get older and
cause breaks with reality. This can lead to delusional thinking, with
people setting up thought processes that aren't connected to reality,
yet they believe in them. They can also have auditory hallucinations—
hearing things that aren't there. These people can be highly intelligent
and can appear to be quite normal, but they live in other worlds and
they're fearful of things that don't exist.

"Most people with these symptoms are not as high functioning and
organized as James Holmes was and they're obviously not in PhD programs. As a neurologist, the social issues around insanity trouble me
because I'm very aware of the way the brain and brain diseases work
and how they can cause behaviors that society believes are criminal.

I've seen people with Alzheimer's become highly disinhibited and do violent things because of the disease. How do we handle that as a culture? Is this criminal behavior or mental illness?

"I see a lot of patients with psychiatric problems who go into talk therapy, as Holmes did, but in my opinion this isn't a very effective treatment. It often doesn't help them understand themselves better or help them cope. Hindsight is 20/20 when looking at people who actually do harmful things. Over the years, I've been threatened by many patients, but I've only been physically attacked on one occasion. It's very difficult to know when you need to commit someone to an institution or to have them held by the authorities.

"In the Holmes case, the question of sanity or insanity comes down to him knowing the difference between right and wrong at the time of the crime. In my view, based upon what I've observed about him from a distance, Holmes is delusional. That's the key thing. He has no motive for doing what he did—none whatsoever. Talk to psychotic people and you'll find no motive for the things they do. We try to apply rational thinking to them and it doesn't work. I've learned to accept that they just have a broken brain.

"To me, it's surprising that these mass shootings don't happen more often. I see a lot of people who are psychotic and have homicidal thoughts, but they don't carry them out. Holmes had the intelligence and the organization to follow through. Drinking and taking drugs, especially in combination, can also help cause people to do these things. They self-medicate excessively or they're bipolar, but they don't take their prescribed drugs because they don't like them— the side effects can dull them out. To be in a manic state can be very pleasurable because it makes people feel creative and smart. With schizophrenia you tend to be in neutral more of the time. That's why it's much harder to pick out someone with this illness."

■　■　■

Just after midnight on July 20, 2012, Holmes set in motion some of the most disturbing questions a society can face. What is criminal insanity? Is it a fixed mental condition or is it, as psychiatrists like to say, "state-dependent?" Are you only insane from time to time and under certain circumstances? The rest of the time you could be sane and relatively normal. What is the liability of psychiatrists and/or universities when they fail to identify and stop a murderous patient and student? Who deserves the death penalty? What impact do violent video games, violent movies, and America's culture of violence, with its eleven-thousand-plus gun murders a year, have on young males?

What are the lasting effects of being bullied, especially in the first years of entering school? What are the long-term consequences of the parent/child relationship, when that connection seems at best tenuous and at worst broken as the child enters maturity and leaves home? Does neuroscience have anything of significance to tell us about what we call "evil" or the criminal mind?

XVII

At Holmes's first courtroom appearance on July 23, he sat next to his lawyer, Tamara Brady, the chief trial deputy for the Colorado Public Defender's office. The photo of them side-by-side that day would become an iconic image of the massacre. With his outlandish curly orange hair and glazed eyes, he looked absent. She looked in shock. Brady and the other lead defense attorney, Daniel King, were members of the Public Defender's death penalty team, as this was likely to turn into a capital punishment case. In 2006, King had defended Sir Mario Owens, who was found guilty of murdering a pair of witnesses testifying against him and sentenced to death row. Now they were faced with defending an even more notorious client.

Observing the dulled-out Holmes in court was haunting for several reasons. His murderous plans had unfolded not on society's fringes, but in the very heart of a medical and psychiatric community devoted to understanding science and human behavior—and using that knowledge to improve our lot. Within the past eighteen months, Holmes had written when applying to graduate school, "Rational people act based on incentives for self-fulfillment, including fulfilling needs of self-development and needs of feeling useful and helpful to others . . . I look forward to fulfilling my quest to advance my knowledge, and I plan to use my critical thinking skills by studying the subject I am passionate about, neuroscience." If his AR-15 had not jammed after thirty seconds, but kept working properly inside Theater Nine, no one could estimate how many others would have been maimed or killed.

Despite her previous experience with death penalty cases, Tamara Brady appeared stunned at finding herself in these circumstances. The lingering terror of the shootings was not just all over the faces of the victims' relatives present in the courtroom, but stamped into the corners of Brady's downturned mouth and lodged in the strain in her eyes. She'd been handed the case less than seventy-two hours earlier and, like everyone else, was trying to make sense of it. Her expression told you that it already was a very lonely job.

"You just can't imagine," says a private detective who's worked on capital punishment cases in the Denver area for decades, "what it's like to be in the position the defense lawyers are in after these mass shootings or other horrific crimes. While everyone else is focused on the police work and the victims, as they should be, the attorneys have a job to do under the law. They're sitting just a few feet away from the victims' families in the courtroom. They're extremely aware of the suffering and loss those families are going through. They're also highly aware of how much the public despises them for stepping in and offering the best legal representation they can to someone like James Holmes.

"They know that some people want to kill their client. They know that some people probably want to kill them. They can't go anywhere without being asked about what they do for a living and why they do it and how can they live with themselves for doing it. In spite of what anyone thinks about them, they feel the tragedy that they're now a part of. There's no group of people involved in these events who are immune to the suffering. I feel for the victim's families and for everyone else in this case."

Brady's eyes conveyed that what had happened three days ago at Century 16 wasn't merely a crime, but a reflection of something more pervasive and disturbing running beneath American society. It reflected a new kind of violence, which some called terrorism, and a new emotional reality that had become normalized so quickly and so completely that it was easy to overlook. That reality was not just individual, but deeply social.

To experience it, all one had to do was click onto a hate-filled website or tune into an AM radio station or a cable-TV talk show and listen to hosts, guests, and callers tear apart people they'd never met and knew virtually nothing about. Under the First Amendment, they were free to proclaim their vitriol against anyone, free to accuse them of all manner of evil or criminal behavior—rape or child molestation or murder—regardless of the truth of any of these projections. Opinions now ruled and facts were irrelevant. Self-expression was all that mattered, regardless of what one was expressing. Venting and being "right" overrode every other consideration.

The producers of these shows often prodded guests and callers to engage in such demonizing because it made for more heated programming, which yielded better ratings, which made more money for everyone. In the past two decades, the nation had seen a bull market in public hatred and this had filtered down into every corner of our national life, from the media to religion to politics to heated daily interactions on sidewalks and street corners—and on into the hallways of colleges and secondary and primary schools. What had once been unacceptable was not merely acceptable now, but encouraged, promoted, pandered to, packaged, sold, and highly rewarded.

Conflict had become a commodity, something to be publicly bought and sold in the media marketplace. Divide the population, start a ferocious argument that no one can win, turn up the heat, sit back, watch the sparks fly, and cash in. Common ground was a quaint thing of the past . . . the object now was to win the argument, and there were no consequences for any of this behavior.

It really had no meaning at all, right? It was just part of the new entertainment industry, wasn't it?

■ ■ ■

This ongoing war was intimate and intensely divisive—and by the first decade of the new millennium it had lasted nearly forty years, compared to the four years of the first American Civil War. No one was unaffected by this new emotional environment and no one could really escape it. While it had overtaken the cultural landscape, there was virtually nothing to counterbalance it—not even much awareness of how pervasive it had become—let alone a strategy for dealing with this fundamental change in our national life. If it was more difficult now for the "well-adjusted" individual to cope in this environment, what about the at-risk population?

The look in Tamara Brady's eyes conjured up something like "mass shame"—and the sense that we were all somehow involved in these shootings, which kept happening again and again. The killers went undetected until it was too late, with law enforcement, psychiatrists, and the "expert" talking heads on television a beat or two behind them. The murders were so destructive and so incomprehensible that they transcended the legal system itself. The Aurora case wasn't just about guilt or innocence, or about crime and punishment, or about sanity or insanity, but about trying to discover something about ourselves we hadn't yet uncovered.

When the case began, the main questions were: Could the legal process help us understand more about the killer and the kind of violence he'd just unleashed? Would his spiral notebook give us insight into what had caused his descent into mass murder? Or would the legal process itself reflect back to us a larger problem?

As the courtroom proceedings unwound week after week, month after month, and then year after year, Brady's face began to change and harden. She was committed to preserving Holmes's doctor-patient confidentiality—and to keeping the spiral notebook away from the prosecution and public. The defense team also surmised that the DA's office would one day make this a death penalty case (the prosecutors had gradually begun gathering input on this issue from eight hundred people who were either survivors of the massacre, or their relatives, or the kin of the deceased). If Holmes's lawyers could do little or nothing to challenge his actual guilt as the shooter, they could fully commit themselves to saving his life. And they'd do so with a ferocity rarely seen before.

In one courtroom exchange with Aurora Police Detective Craig Appel, Brady brought up Appel's questioning of Holmes on the day of the crime.

"Did you," she asked, "tell him what he [Holmes] was telling you could be used to put him to death?"

With weariness and resignation, Appel replied, "There was too much death that day."

While his attorneys fought in court for the defendant and Holmes sat beside them and stared into his lap, the victims' relatives began a ritual that would continue through 2012, into 2013, and still beyond, leaning against one another and stifling tears or not being able to; stroking or rubbing one another's backs, shoulders, arms, and hair; constantly touching each other for connection and comfort, while trying not to say anything out loud or make any extraneous noises, as they struggled to contain their feelings for the young man sitting just a few feet away. Almost all of the time, they succeeded.

During one hearing, Steve Hernandez, the father of victim Rebecca Wingo, cried out, "Rot in hell, Holmes!" The judge reprimanded Hernandez, but not very strongly, as if he understood the man's plight.

The defendant would be charged with twenty-four counts of first-degree murder and 142 counts of attempted murder. His oldest homicide victim was fifty-one, while the youngest was six (the youngest survivor hit by gunfire was four months old). Following the rampage, some of the victims had been so bloodied that emergency medical personnel could not immediately tell if they were young or old, male or female, black or white. In spite of the horror at Century 16, and in spite of President Obama's visit to Aurora right after the shootings, and in spite of the growing sense that this violent phenomenon had to be addressed at the highest levels of our government, the

U.S. Congress wasn't quite ready to introduce legislation regarding what an untrained civilian with an AR-15 and hundreds of rounds of ammunition could do in a crowded venue in less than one minute.

The sound of Holmes opening fire in the theater had been captured on audio and would be played in open court. It was the closest one could come to the feeling of being trapped in front of a semiautomatic rifle, without actually being there. While the victims' relatives grieved and buried their loved ones, the survivors faced unmanageable medical bills (although local hospitals did waive some of the costs). They'd soon be publically fighting with the authorities over how to distribute the money raised to assist them.

XVIII

We'd noted that after these mass tragedies, the media commentators were almost always middle aged or older. Young men and women of Eric's generation were rarely asked about these events. "That's why my friends don't get their news from your media, like CNN, Fox, or MSNBC," Eric said. Instead they went to the Internet and visited sites like TruthOut, AlterNet, and Vice. "The people who run the mainstream media," he said, "are also too old to understand."

In December 2014, the Nielsen ratings showed that over the last three years, viewership of traditional programming by eighteen- to twenty-four-year-olds had declined by almost 22 percent. Turning away from conventional television, this age bracket had begun tuning in to the Internet and a host of news portals such as Vice.com and other alternate sites. In 1994, *Vice* was founded in Montreal by Suroosh Alvi, Shane Smith, and Gavin McInnes. It debuted as an international magazine focused on news, arts, and general culture, but later expanded into Vice Media, offering a website, record label, film production company, and publishing imprint. From the beginning, it had a well-defined mission. Back in the 1960s, a group of mostly East Coast reporters had come up with New Journalism, in which a writer approached a topic with more personal involvement and offered readers more of a point of view, instead of constantly trying to remain objective. The *Vice* editors took this concept a step further, with the idea of "Immersion" journalism. Its reporters went to places most other journalists ignored and became involved with the people they were covering in a more hands-on way. *Vice* operated with an attitude that was certain to disturb, if not offend, some other journalists and parts of the mainstream media.

In 1999, *Vice* relocated to New York City and began moving away from general culture and taking on more weighty subjects. Whole issues or programs were devoted to the lives of the Iraqi people, the Russian people, Native Americans, or people struggling with mental disorders and mental disabilities. In 2007, founder Suroosh Alvi defined the Vice credo in an interview with *Wired* magazine: "Traditional journalism always aspires to objectivity, and since day one with the magazine we never believed in that . . . Our ethos is subjectivity with real substantiation. I don't think you see that on CNN."

Vice Films was created in a deal between MTV Networks and the Logo Group. In March 2007, MTV funded the VBS.tv network, and *Vice* magazine began supplying the content for the films. Vice.com was soon putting out short, highly provocative, award-winning documentaries that showed up on YouTube and other platforms, like HBO. For one program, Vice Films sent a reporter into the most dangerous neighborhoods in Chicago to interview local gang members, who referred to their part of the Windy City as "Chiraq." When the reporter asked those gathered round him on a nighttime street corner if they were armed, everyone pulled out a gun. The look on his face was not something one was likely to see on any of the major networks.

Another Vice Film demonstrated how 3-D printers could be used to create one's own supply of weapons. Another followed a thrash metal band around Iraq and delved into the mounting refugee crisis in Syria. Another documented a heroin epidemic in England, and another sent a correspondent into the South American jungles to experiment with some local psychotropic drugs. He didn't report on them; he took them.

In 2013, *Vice* shocked parts of the media by announcing in mid-August that 21st Century Fox, owned by Rupert Murdoch, had invested $70 million in Vice Media, giving Fox a 5 percent stake in the company. Following the consummation of the deal, founder Shane Smith told *The Guardian* that "we have set ourselves up to build a global platform but we have maintained control."

If *Vice* inevitably put off some older and more traditional journalists and their employers because of its embrace of subjectivity, it had clearly found an audience among the young, whose mistrust of mainstream media was one part of a larger mistrust of American society, politics, and culture.

From a twenty-one-year-old male from Seattle:

Vice is important because it hasn't marketed itself to older people. It's aimed at the young as a different way of getting the news and staying aware of what's going on in the world. It's meant to get and to hold the attention of viewers my age, the same age as all the people who are being diagnosed with attention deficit disorder. Vice has adapted to who we are. It does this by using catchy graphics and film techniques. My friends won't sit down and watch 60 Minutes *or sixty minutes of most anything on TV. But we'll watch ten- to fifteen-minute segments of a documentary about some guy who goes to some risky place and puts his ass on the line to get a story. That's someone I can respect. These CNN and Fox reporters seem dulled out and numb.*

XIX

Being numb was something Denver had experienced well before the tragedy in Aurora. On a chilly, windy, damp evening in late April 1999, we'd left five-year-old Eric with a babysitter and driven out to Columbine High School in southwestern Denver, where hundreds upon hundreds of teenagers and adults had come to grieve, kneeling down in the cold spring mud and bursting into tears or grabbing onto one another for support or clutching a metal fence and swaying as they wailed. Red Cross and Salvation Army trucks hummed nearby, conjuring up a war zone.

A few days before, Columbine seniors Eric Harris and Dylan Klebold had walked into the school and opened fire with shotguns and semiautomatic weapons, wounding twenty-three students and killing twelve teenagers, one teacher, and themselves in the worst high school shooting in American history.

Like Holmes, they'd been dressed for and committed to all-out combat, but their rage was aimed directly at the educational system, which they felt had mistreated them for years. They'd been openly bullied in Columbine's hallways and finally decided to bully the bully, regardless of who got harmed or killed. The victimization they'd known by merely attending school would now be felt by everyone.

They'd built ninety-five bombs and planted most of them around Columbine. Some were intended to detonate inside the school cafeteria at 11:20 a.m., during the height of lunch hour, so that hundreds of kids would die while eating. When the survivors came running outside to escape the fireballs, the two young men would be strategically placed to gun them down. The bombs and bullets were supposed to kill five hundred people, maybe more, and to dwarf the 1993 Oklahoma City bombing, which had left 168 dead.

When the explosives failed to go off and the plan went awry, the young men entered the school and began shooting.

They'd very consciously chosen their day of infamy—April 20, 1999—because it was Adolf Hitler's 110th birthday. The purpose of the bloodbath, revealed on a videotape discovered after the killers were dead, was also worthy of Hitler. It was meant to "kick-start a revolution" against their enemies: "niggers, spics, Jews, gays, fucking whites . . . humanity."

As Harris had written in his diary leading up to the massacre, "Everyone is making fun of me because of how I look, how fucking weak I am, and shit, well I will get you all back, ultimate fucking revenge here. You people could have shown more respect, treated me better, asked for more knowledge or guidance, treated me more like a senior, and maybe I wouldn't have been so ready to tear your fucking heads off . . .

"Same thing with all those rich snotty toadies at my school. Fuckers think they are higher than me and everyone else with all their $ just because they were born into it?"

In a videotape made in Harris's bedroom roughly a month before the tragedy, they passed a bottle of whiskey back and forth and talked about the upcoming slaughter. Their calmness and lucidity were startling, as were their lengthy apologies to their parents for the carnage that was coming. They weren't angry at how their parents had raised them; they were enraged at the culture they found themselves living in as they'd gotten older and moved through the educational system.

"It fucking sucks to do this to them," Harris said about his mother and father. "They're going to be put through hell once we do this . . . There's nothing you guys could've done to prevent this."

Klebold told his mom and dad that they'd been "great parents" who'd taught him "self-awareness, self-reliance . . . I always appreciated that." He paused and said, "I'm sorry I have so much rage."

"My parents are the best fucking parents I have ever known," Harris said. "My dad is great. I wish I was a fucking sociopath so I didn't have any remorse, but I do." He spoke just as lovingly of his mother: "I really am sorry about all this." And then he put into words what seemed to be the driving force and the driving belief system behind one mass shooting after another: "But war's war."

And like many other soldiers, or terrorists, they were willing to sacrifice their lives for their convictions. Earlier American wars had been with only external enemies. At Columbine, the war had come home. Now the battle was against one's classmates—or oneself.

Before the April 20 attack, the boys expressed their longstanding hatred toward several groups and individuals within the high school. "You've given us shit for years," Klebold said of his classmates. "You're fucking going to pay for all the shit. We don't give a shit because we're going to die doing it." The problems, Klebold went on, were much broader than what they'd encountered at the school. They included all of "humanity. Look at what you made. You're fucking shit, you humans, and you need to die."

"We need to die too," Harris said.

After entering the Columbine library, but before opening fire, Harris said to the cowering students, "Everyone with white hats [worn by those on Columbine sports teams], stand up! This is for all the shit you've given us for the past four years! All jocks stand up! We'll get the guys in white hats!"

In the weeks following the massacre, the National Safety Center reported that three thousand other high school students around the country had lately concocted bomb threats or violent schemes intended to result in death. Some adults were starting to get the message—that the discontent among the young was more widespread than just those who exploded into mass violence.

"If I hear one more teenager say that he or she understands why those two kids did what they did at Columbine," a veteran journalist remarked in the aftermath of the shootings, "I'm going to scream. I don't understand them."

■ ■ ■

After Columbine, as more and more shootings accumulated around the country, the conversation gradually expanded to include the adolescent or young adult brain. Childhood trauma—and how psychopaths could be created as a result of it—was just beginning to be studied in depth.

"Your brain's wiring," says a neuroscientist at Anschutz, "gets put together as you grow up and go through your personal experiences. Ninety-nine percent of the connections of the nerve cells haven't yet been made when you're born. They get connected through time. If you have a traumatic and fearful event when you're young, all you need as an adult is for something to trigger that memory and then that piece of wiring in the brain gets activated. It's already imprinted on your brain circuitry.

"What you felt in the first or second grade is still there, waiting to be felt again and waiting to re-traumatize you. If you were bullied as a child, the wiring for that experience is still in place. All it takes it to be triggered."

For years, the authorities handling the Columbine investigation did everything they could to keep the videos made by Harris and Klebold in the lead-up to the crime from being released. Some in the psychiatric community argued that this evidence should be suppressed to keep the killers from being mythologized, but others contended that it needed to be disseminated and used to study young mass shooters. Like the spiral notebook, the videos were at the heart of this ongoing debate. Was it better to look openly at all the available evidence or to turn away from it? Was it better to examine the full reality or to bury it? There was no indication that ignoring the evidence had lessened the mass-shooting phenomenon.

From a twenty-one-year-old female college student in Washington, DC:

I lived in Denver at the time of Columbine, but was too young to under-stand it. But I can still remember the feeling of that day, the shock that everyone was going through. Thirteen years later, I was out of the country when Aurora happened. This time I really felt for my community and was sorry I couldn't be there with people, especially people my age. These things have become so normalized in our society—so commonplace—but the feelings they leave behind never go away.

My peers have a political perspective on everything in our culture, including strengthening the gun laws. Every new shooting sets off a new round of discussions about this. We just don't understand why we can't get older people to move on these things and to make some real changes.

I go to school in Washington, DC, and was there recently when the mothers of the Newtown victims came to the Capitol. They tried to get the House and Senate to pass gun control bills, but failed. They were helpless to make this happen. What's it going to take to wake people up? How many more of these events do we need? I hate to say this, but my friends and I have been exposed to so much of this violence that it's no longer a big deal. At the same time, we feel nervous. I look at people I know who are not happy and I wonder what they're capable of.

I think: How dangerous are they, really?

XX

Harris and Klebold had purchased their weapons from private dealers at a firearms show. Following Columbine, President Bill Clinton called for more gun control legislation, and in May 1999 the Senate narrowly passed an amendment requiring background checks on all private dealer sales at gun shows. In a burst of optimism, Senator Chuck Schumer (D-NY) declared victory over the gun lobby.

"It will never be the same again," he said. "The vise lock that the NRA [National Rifle Association] has had on the Senate and the House is broken."

He seemed to have a point. After the horror at Columbine, the NRA itself said their organization was open to more regulation, admitting in an ad campaign: "It's reasonable to provide for instant background checks at gun shows, just like gun stores and pawnshops."

Then the NRA launched a major lobbying effort to kill such checks. In the two months leading up to the final 1999 Congressional vote, the group spent $1.5 million toward this end and threatened dangerous consequences for the nation if the background checks were approved. The bill failed.

In the coming years, the gun lobby would spend nearly $660,000 in Colorado to derail numerous state gun control laws. A few minor bills *were* passed, one of them allowing for the arrest of people who buy guns for criminals and children, and another reauthorizing a state background-check program. But legislation requiring background checks at gun shows, safe storage of guns inside of homes, and an increase from age eighteen to twenty-one for buying a handgun were all defeated.

Thirteen years and thirty-one mass shootings later—counting Holmes's rampage in Aurora—80 percent of crime guns were still purchased via private dealers and without a background check. By the close of 2012, following both the Aurora and Newtown massacres, some U.S. politicians were again poised to address gun control legislation. A bill limiting the sale of online ammunition, filed by Senators Frank Lautenberg (D-NJ) and Representative Carolyn McCarthy (D-NY), was introduced in the House in January 2013, a few weeks after the Sandy Hook tragedy and during the period when people were saying that the events at Newtown had finally caused America to reach its tipping point when it came to legislating tighter gun controls.

The proposed 2013 bill would dramatically curb one's ability to buy unlimited rounds of ammunition through mail orders or the Internet, as Holmes had done, by requiring a photo ID at the time of purchase. It also required ammo dealers to report bulk sales to law enforcement. The bill failed to muster the filibuster-proof sixty votes even to get through the Senate—*after* polls repeatedly stated that 90 percent of the American people supported it.

Following this latest defeat for gun control advocates, the NRA held its annual convention in Houston, featuring a company that sold shooting targets "designed to help YOU prepare for the upcoming Zombie outbreak." It also offered consumers an "Ex-Girlfriend" target that bled when you shot it. The more bullets you put into the target, the more mangled the once-attractive body became (among the copious statistics surrounding women and violence is that a woman's chances of being killed by her male abuser go up more than seven times if he has access to a firearm).

In Colorado in 2013, state Senate President John Morse and state Senator Angela Giron were ousted in recall votes for supporting stricter gun control laws. The successful campaign against them was named "Ready, Aim, Fired." The man elected to replace John Morse, Republican State Senator Bernie Herpin, gained notoriety at a Colorado legislative hearing on overturning a ban on gun magazines of fifteen rounds or more. The Republican supported getting rid of this ban so shooters could have *larger* magazines.

"My understanding," Senator Irene Aguilar said to Herpin during the hearing, "is that James Holmes bought his 100-round capacity magazine legally. So in fact, this law would have stopped James Holmes from purchasing a 100-round magazine. I was wondering if you agree with me."

"Perhaps," Herpin responded, "James Holmes would not have been able to purchase a 100-round magazine. As it turned out, that was maybe a good thing that he had a 100-round magazine, because it jammed. If he had four, five, six, fifteen-round magazines, there's no telling how much damage he could have done until a good guy with a gun showed up."

Attending this hearing was Tom Sullivan, whose son, Alex, had been killed at Century 16. When called upon to testify, Sullivan said, "I've had a lot of thoughts since July 20, 2012, but never once did I think anyone was better off because the shooter brought a hundred round drum into that theater. Alex never had a chance. He was watching a movie one second and the next he was dead. The fact is, if the shooter had to change his magazine that would have been a chance for Alex to survive."

Later, when interviewed by Denver's Fox-31 TV station, Sullivan added, "The lack of empathy and compassion is shocking. Not just to me and my family, but to all of the families who have lost loved ones to gun violence and to all the people of Colorado. But this is what he [Herpin] truly believes. And to think this is the person who they brought in to replace John Morse."

Rather than acting as a tipping point for more gun control, Sandy Hook seemed to bolster those arguing the opposite view.

From a twenty-nine-year-old male medical student in Philadelphia:

> People who are now in their fifties and sixties used to believe in social and political change, but they've completely given this up. I don't understand that, but I see and feel the effects of it all around me. The mass support that once existed for this kind of change is gone and a lot of the cynicism in our culture flows from this. There's a sense that nothing good can happen now, that nothing will get better, and that you're confronting all this without any social support. Our elections are a sham and our leaders are basically powerless in terms of getting anything done. President Obama is a good man, but that doesn't seem to make any difference.
>
> People talk about feeling pride in your country, but I've never felt that and neither has anyone I know. In some ways, my feelings are hypocritical because I benefit from this society economically, compared to so many others in the world, but I'm not proud of that. Our whole society is about getting lots of things for yourself—period. TV ads tell you to take the path of least resistance, and to get all you can now, and many people do exactly that. It's why the culture feels so incredibly hollow.

Interlude

The more our son used words like *isolation*, *escape*, and *dystopian*, the more we compared his coming of age with earlier periods of American history. Our two fathers had both been part of the battle against fascism in World War II. Like others of the baby boomer generation, we'd both grown up connected to major social/political movements— for racial equality, gender equality, and protesting against the Vietnam War—that were far larger than we were as individuals. For our parents and for us, all of these events had occurred within a moral framework. Defeating Hitler was a necessity. Attempting to defeat racism, expand human rights, and end a war that tens of millions of people saw as unjust was as well. The political movements of our youth enforced and reinforced one's sense of being a member of society with an obligation to fight the just fight. If you participated in them, even in small ways, you were not only supported by huge portions of the culture, but you felt that you were serving the public interest, the common good. Most people who were a part of such movements carried some piece of this with them into the coming decades.

All of this seemed rather obvious—until we began listening to what our son and a number of millennials were telling us. They spoke a lot about the need for social change, but there was little in their culture that provided a framework for these convictions. You could surf the Internet and find small groups who backed anything you felt or believed in, but that wasn't the same thing as a mass march on Washington or a protest at the Pentagon. At age twenty, it seemed to us, Eric had never taken part in anything that he was certain served a larger or a moral cause. He hadn't grown up with clear-cut public role models in politics, the media, religion, or elsewhere. For many young people now, he told us more than once, the only such models were action heroes in movies or musicians or sports figures.

And what recent American history had the millennials lived through? What series of events had characterized the formative years of their generation?

As they were becoming more aware of the society they were living in, and as mass shootings began to accumulate into what some called an "epidemic," the United States was passing through an unprecedented national era. Between 2001 and 2014, our country had come to accept certain things as normal: that a state of war with other parts of the world was a permanent reality; that we could incarcerate (and torture) people indefinitely without giving them due process of law; that all of us—the entire population—was under constant surveillance by our own government; that America was roughly $17 trillion in debt, partly as a result of these wars and that spying; that in the first three months of 2014, the United States saw more than 1,800 of its veterans, many from the current wars, commit suicide; that no one in power, from the top down, had talked about any of this freely or openly in public; and finally, and most importantly, that in the face of these highly complex realities, violence was constantly promoted as the best, if not the only, solution.

■ ■ ■

"The United States has a lot of built-in cultural violence," says Mitchell Hall, a Holistic Health & Wellness coordinator and counselor at PsycheHealth, Ltd., in the San Francisco Bay area. "We are by far the most violent developed country in the western world, with ten to twenty times the murder rate of most other similar countries. You can't divorce these numbers from our political and economic atmosphere. About half of our annual budget as a country goes to the military for warfare. This is our daily reality, the backdrop of our national life. We are paying for the wars of an empire and they are being fought on behalf of that empire. We invade other countries and lies are told to support this.

"Young people see all of the corruption and feel cynicism and despair because they don't think they have the power to do anything about it. Someone like James Holmes comes along and develops a fantasy of having power, instead of having any actual power over himself or his own life. He was going to make a contribution to neuroscience, until his megalomania took over.

"The changes in our culture need to be systemic. One percent of the American population controls most of the wealth. The people running America are overextended and can't offer social services to the population. The ruling elite have ever more pervasive means for maintaining this power game and for not setting up a more just society. It all adds up to trouble and it all filters down to the young. Change needs to come on so many levels and in so many domains. The violence of the young keeps telling us this."

Somebody once said of Ernest Hemingway that he just pointed out what was obvious. And someone else who was more astute said, "Yes, but it only became obvious *after* he pointed it out." Something like that process was happening now between us and the millennials we spoke to.

It took us a while to understand what we were hearing from many different angles about our current culture and about how things had changed since when we'd grown up. Then the contrasts began to stand out. In the 1970s, Steve had become a reporter in part because of the Watergate scandal. That event had brought to public awareness a pair of hard-working, courageous, nationally recognized journalistic role models whom one could aspire to learn from and emulate. As important as the reporters themselves, Bob Woodward and Carl Bernstein, were the editors of *The Washington Post* who did not buckle under to pressure from politicians to stop their Watergate investigation.

As a result, abuses of power at the highest levels of government were identified, and serious attempts were made to correct them. People who'd violated the U.S. Constitution or the law went to jail. They were forced to pay the price for lying and deceiving the American population. The truth behind significant corruption came out in very large and very public ways. The press, the Congress, and the judicial branch of government all came together to right a wrong and clean out the stables in Washington. The system worked.

That kind of investigative journalism, supported by the muscle of a major American newspaper, has more or less faded in recent decades. Whistleblowers like Julian Assange of WikiLeaks and Edward Snowden who had revealed government spying programs were now accused of crimes by the federal government and were more or less left to face the charges on their own.

What Eric and his friends now had when it came to uncovering the reality behind huge political events was the Internet, with its thousand-plus variations of the truth. And unlike in Watergate, there was very little social and political support for finding that reality. If there were high-ranking American officials who'd engaged in bad behavior in the past thirteen years—or criminal behavior—there had to date been no consequences for them of any kind. One could hardly blame twenty somethings for being cynical or questioning whether their votes even mattered.

People of our son's generation did not trust the media or the government or any other social institution to ferret out the facts behind our recent history and do something constructive with them. Young people had never actually seen these various safeguarding components work in unison to root out abuse, maintain a balance of power, and serve the overriding public good. Their experience was all about watching a society divide itself against itself, in red versus blue states, the right versus the left, my side is right and yours is wrong. This dynamic now pervaded every aspect of American life, in politics, religion, the media, and the general culture.

Some would argue that these problems had always been with us, and that there was nothing new about what had unfolded in America in the past twenty years. They may have been right, but only up to a point. In earlier times, wars and mass surveillance in the United States had come and gone, but they'd often been met with significant protest. What was different now was that our rich national tradition of dissent—of the questioning of authority by citizens—had all but disappeared, except on the fringes. The fringes were vital and necessary, but rarely impacted mainstream politics and media.

We've quietly and passively accepted this new political and emotional reality, largely based upon the constant sense of looming disaster. We tout ourselves as the most powerful nation on earth, but we are always about to be attacked or crushed by some force that is worse than anything America had endured in the past. We are always about to be victimized by something beyond our control—a mindset that had not applied when we were defeating Nazi Germany or Imperial Japan (in just over three and a half years), or sending a man to the moon (in just over eight years), or fighting for equal rights for all citizens.

While all of this raised many issues and questions, one in particular begged to be addressed: What had these developments and this atmosphere wrought on those born in the late 1980s and 1990s?

■ ■ ■

When Eric was visiting from college, he told us a story about how after September 11, 2001, the administration of a prominent liberal university in the western United States had sent out a directive to its faculty: Because of the sensitivity of this event, the directive said, refrain from talking about it in the classroom. This information had been relayed to Eric by a professor who was given the directive, and years later the teacher was still affected by it.

"What this really does is undermine critical thought," the professor had said to Eric. "The whole point of a discipline like political science or history or sociology is to do exactly the opposite. When something like this happens, it makes critical thinkers start to worry about the reach of power on campuses. It puts a chill on the kind of environment that saw the Free Speech Movement and the war protests of the 1960s. Power can be measured by the limits of what is allowed to be talked about."

The firmness of this order came as a shock to numerous instructors, but they obeyed. Doing otherwise was too risky, yet some never forgot the feeling of being told to keep silent about things that changed the course of United States, if not world, history.

One of them later said, "Talking about what's happening in our society is what we do. It made me question my job and my value as an educator. A university is supposed to be a sanctuary for critical thought."

■ ■ ■

The ban on open public discourse lasted for a very long time. In December 2014, more than thirteen years after this directive came down, the Senate Select Intelligence Committee released a 534-page report—the first-ever public accounting of the CIA's use of torture on al-Qaida detainees held in secret facilities in Europe and Asia after September 11, 2001. We could finally talk in the media and beyond, and we could finally think critically about what had unfolded in secret "black sites" around the world, under orders from the American government. We could at last consider the cost of all this officially sanctioned violence, from the top down.

Only days after this report was released, Carl Levin, Chairman of the Senate Armed Services Committee, brought forth more information that he pointed to as evidence that the Bush Administration had willfully misled the nation in the run-up to the war in Iraq. Speaking on the Senate floor, Levin outlined a 2003 CIA cable warning the George W. Bush administration *against* making claims that Mohammad Atta, the leader of the 9/11 hijackers, had met with an Iraqi intelligence officer in the Czech Republic before September 11, 2001. Instead of taking this advice, Levin stated, Bush officials used this unconfirmed meeting to link Iraq to 9/11 and thereby to justify the U.S. invasion of Iraq.

"There was," Levin said, "a concerted campaign on the part of the Bush administration to connect Iraq in the public mind with the horror of the September 11 attacks. That campaign succeeded." He cited opinion polls from that time demonstrating that many Americans believed that former Iraqi leader Saddam Hussein was involved in the attacks on the United States. "Of course," Levin said, "connections between Saddam and 9/11 or al-Qaida were fiction."

These two Senate actions, coming back to back, were a sea change from the collective passivity that had preceded them for more than a decade. Was it possible that the dam of fear and silence was finally cracking and falling apart?

On December 22, 2014, *The New York Times* editorial board went even further, calling for an investigation and prosecution of those in the George W. Bush administration who sanctioned torture. The board wrote, "Starting a criminal investigation is not about payback; it is about ensuring that this never happens again and regaining the moral credibility to rebuke torture by other governments. Because of the Senate's report, we now know the distance officials in the executive branch went to rationalize, and conceal, the crimes they wanted to commit. The question is whether the nation will stand by and allow the perpetrators of torture to have perpetual immunity for their actions."

Nothing like this had ever happened before in our son's lifetime. The adult world had finally started to puncture the moral vacuum, a desolate space that included James Holmes.

"JUSTICE IS DEATH"

XXI

Suburban sprawl has eaten up more and more acres southeast of Denver, but the countryside opens up as you approach the Arapahoe County Justice Center from the west. In the modest hills around the Center, prairie dogs dart in and out of the holes they've dug in the beige dirt for their underground refuges. Geese float overhead, hawks circle for prey, and coyotes roam the ridges, causing the prairie dogs to once again dive beneath the earth. Next door is Dove Valley, home of the Denver Broncos football team, for decades the biggest rallying cry in a city that's hungered for—and occasionally received—national glory in the realm of professional sports. Days before the massacre, Holmes had sat in an Aurora bar, discussing the Broncos' upcoming season with some other fans. The team had recently signed superstar quarterback Peyton Manning, and the town was abuzz.

Only one person in the tavern knew that an even larger piece of news was about to break in Denver. By gunning down twelve people at the Century 16 complex, injuring seventy more, and then surrendering to the police, Holmes would launch an endless set of new alliances and connections, including support groups for the victims; the coming together of anti-death penalty allies; the emergence of young men and women called "Holmies" who were drawn to the killer, with some females expressing a romantic interest in him; and worldwide followers of the case who quickly found one another online.

Subcultures and conspiracies sprung up around the tragedy and all of their attention was focused on the Arapahoe County Justice Center and Courtroom 201, where Judge William Sylvester presided. What would the legal system do with former PhD candidate James Eagan Holmes?

Months passed as he waited for the legal process to grind forward. His defense had made no plea of any kind, as if they were waiting for the judge to force them into taking action. Living in his cell in isolation, Holmes became heavier, more pale, with even duller eyes. He wore a beard, grew his dark brown hair longer, and began slicking it back, the orange-red hues now gone. Like most incarcerated people, he began to look more and more like a prisoner. Each time he came into court, he seemed to have deteriorated further—nothing like "Jimmy James," the bright-eyed, slightly mischievous-appearing young man who'd snapped close-up pictures of himself right before the killings.

During the hearings, he didn't move for hours, sometimes not even shifting in his chair at the defense table. He never glanced at anyone in the gallery or acted as if he were listening to testimony. His earlier, more buoyant self had been enfolded by a thickening lump of flesh that conveyed the notion, whether by design or not, of someone growing crazier by the minute.

In the courtroom, he seemed unfazed by the barely controlled rage and disgust coming at him from the victims' relatives, which continued throughout the paralyzing heat of the summer of 2012, the battering cold of the winter of 2013, the late spring snowstorms, and the heat of summer again. Nearly a year passed with only minor developments, as fewer and fewer of the victims' kin came to the courthouse to watch the sluggish proceedings. They sat clumped together in the gallery, holding hands and touching shoulders, but crying less often now. They occasionally made disapproving noises, disheartened at how long it was taking to bring Holmes to trial.

As youngsters, they'd all sat through civics classes about how our government and legal system function, but now they were watching that system unfold in front of their eyes. America's founders had understood how easily power could be abused by kings and religious authorities, and they were determined that anyone charged with a crime in the United States would have the right to counsel and to the presumption of innocence until proven guilty.

Due process could be extremely repetitive and tedious. Real courtrooms were nothing like the crime dramas they'd seen on TV throughout their lives, where everything was wrapped up neatly inside of an hour or less. Fictional shows about murder held the same relation to actual homicides that televised violence did to its real-life counterpart. The former was there to entertain you—quickly and seamlessly—while the latter never lost its capacity to shock and sicken.

Surviving victims of crimes also had rights now, and the wounded and the relatives of those killed at the theater were polled on whether the prosecution should pursue the death penalty against Holmes. Or should the DA's office let him plead guilty and resolve the case quickly and at far less public expense? A majority of those who participated in the poll wanted to see the defendant executed.

■ ■ ■

Holmes's parents, Arlene and Robert, occasionally showed up in court, sitting in front of the assembled media and positioned as far away as possible from the victims' relatives. To their immediate right—so that no reporter could slide in next to them and start asking questions— was a court official. Everywhere they went inside the courthouse, he or she ran interference for them. They too were under the strict gag order that Judge Sylvester had imposed three days after the massacre.

Arlene constantly leaned her weight onto her husband, so that their bodies seemed to be growing into one another. They said nothing to strangers, looked directly at no one, kept their eyes down when walking the courthouse halls or visiting the restroom, and displayed no emotion, as if all of this could make them invisible. Several feet in front of them at the defense table, their son wore a red jumpsuit, handcuffs, and shackles on his ankles. Entering the courtroom through a side door before the proceedings started, with two heavily armed guards at his side, Holmes gave his parents a passing nod, and they subtly glanced back at him.

Scattered around the gallery were a few defenders of the accused, the "Holmies" who often showed up at the hearings to offer him support. They tended to wear black and to have multicolored hair. One young woman had dyed her locks bright orange in solidarity with the defendant, back when he was mimicking The Joker. She confided to a reporter that she was attending the proceedings because her brother was bipolar and she felt that Holmes was suffering from the same condition; she was trying to understand more about the illness.

In court, she stared longingly at the young man at the defense table, trying to catch his eye.

"I think I'm in love with him," she acknowledged.

"Why?" she was asked.

"Because he's just so cute."

When her feelings for the defendant became known publicly, she received threats on her Facebook page and soon took it down, but other "Holmie" sites remained in operation.

In January 2013, six months after the massacre, Century16 reopened in Aurora following significant repairs. It offered a weekend of free movies: an obvious effort by the theater to rebuild community trust and goodwill. Even though management had rechristened the complex and remodeled Theater Nine, many who visited that weekend still didn't think the place "felt right." The residue of terror had been left behind—and changing the interior and name of Theater Nine didn't exorcise it.

The first evening of the reopening, all the theaters were packed, but out behind Theater Nine, in the exact spot where Holmes had been arrested following the shootings, a group of his young followers sat in a circle of defiance on the asphalt. Dressed in black goth clothing, they were there to remind everyone that they saw the young man as one more victim of the tragedy.

■ ■ ■

As the wounded and their families, reporters, and courtroom observers waited for something—*anything*—to happen in the case, Colorado politicians responded to the shooting with legislation on mental illness and gun control. Within days of the event, Governor John Hickenlooper and state health officials had begun a dialogue about revamping a mental health system gutted by recent budget cuts. In the past half decade, Colorado hospitals had lost about 110 beds, while several private hospitals had closed their mental health inpatient units and sharply reduced their capacity. Without more beds, the only alternatives were putting mentally ill patients into relatives' homes, taking them to emergency rooms, or locking them up in jail.

"We lobby our local politicians and one of our purposes in doing this is to reduce the stigma around mental health issues," says Don Mares, President and CEO of Mental Health America in Colorado, an affiliate of the MHA's national organization. "It's unfortunate that the mental health conversation has found itself too often mired in these rare violent episodes like the Holmes case. The huge percentage of violence around mental health is perpetrated *on* people with mental health issues, rather than *by* people with these issues."

According to the National Institute of Mental Health, about 6 percent of the population, or one in seventeen Americans, suffers from a serious mental illness. The mentally ill are involved in about 4 percent of violent crimes, but if left untreated, severe mental illness is associated with higher rates of violence.

"We're talking about a society," says Mares, "that needs to have a whole perspective shift on mental health issues and to become more accepting of this reality. People theorize about why suicide rates are higher in Colorado than some other places. In the West, we still tend to tell ourselves, 'I don't need your help. I can handle this alone.' If we can get people talking and acting on these issues, over time we'll start to see a shift."

By mid-December 2012, Governor Hickenlooper was ready to put forth a new Colorado initiative on mental health. His announcement came right after the next incomprehensible massacre—the Sandy Hook elementary school shootings in Newtown, Connecticut.

"The common element of so many of these mass homicides," he said during his speech, "seems to be a level of mental illness."

The Governor eventually signed into law a $20 million expansion of mental health services, including the establishing of walk-in crisis centers across the state, an around-the-clock mental health hotline, and mobile units to go into rural areas with limited mental health resources. He then signed a bill to study ways to consolidate Colorado laws for placing someone in involuntary commitment—like the seventy-two-hour hold not used on Holmes in June 2012—making it easier for judges to act on the need for emergency restraints.

If the legal system had done little so far with the Holmes case, it had made a large enough impact on Denver and the state to stimulate some political change. It had kick-started what had previously been dormant.

"Fifteen or so years ago," says Don Mares, "there was a screaming need around keeping people with mental health problems out of jails and emergency rooms so we developed a crisis response plan for the metro area, a hotline for people in need. Governor Hickenlooper developed a similar plan recently because of the Holmes case. It was modeled after the work we did. This is an odd positive result of what James Holmes did in Aurora."

Colorado lawmakers also approved universal background checks on gun buyers, a ban on firearms purchases by those convicted of domestic violence, and another ban on high-capacity magazines.

In May 2013, Hickenlooper surprised everyone by indefinitely delaying the execution of Nathan Dunlap, scheduled to die three months later by lethal injection. Convicted of the 1993 murder of four Chuck E. Cheese employees, Dunlap was one of Colorado's three death row inmates. All were African American and all had been prosecuted within the same Eighteenth Judicial District that was set to try Holmes. With this decision, Hickenlooper hoped to "start a conversation" about capital punishment in a state where a 2011 poll showed that 47 percent of the people wanted to repeal the death penalty in favor of life without parole, while 47 percent wanted to keep it. He almost lost his 2014 reelection bid, in part because of this position.

■ ■ ■

Because of the legislation passed following the shootings in Aurora and at Sandy Hook Elementary School in Newtown, Colorado now has thirteen walk-in crisis centers statewide. In December 2014, Denver Mayor Michael Hancock appointed Don Mares, the former President and CEO of Mental Health America of Colorado, as Executive Director of Denver's new office of Behavior Health Strategies. This is the first office of its kind in a major U.S. city. One of its potential initiatives would be to train Denver's eleven thousand employees in mental health first aid. Slowly, Colorado was beginning to address the roots of mass violence.

XXII

After nearly eight months of silence from the defense, Judge Sylvester finally grew impatient. The prosecutors and the victims and their relatives, too, felt that Holmes and his defense team were just stalling to buy time—and to keep his spiral notebook and psychiatric history out of the courtroom. Two hundred and fifty days into the case, reputedly no one on either side or the judge had looked at the document that could provide the most accurate window into the defendant's consciousness leading up to the shootings. His state of mind would be the pivotal issue in court. But his writings and drawings had been sealed and locked away, apparently from everyone.

Media attorney Steven Zansberg had never stopped trying to get the judge to lift the gag order enough to give news organizations and the public more information about the massacre. Both the prosecution and defense resisted him, with Public Defender Daniel King telling Judge Sylvester that he did not see the point of having "Mr. Zansberg underfoot" as the case unfolded.

In March 2013, the judge took action, pleading "not guilty" on the defendant's behalf, although the defense still retained the option of changing this plea. Two weeks later, Holmes's lawyers offered a guilty plea and life in prison without parole for their client—if prosecutors would not seek the death penalty against him.

"Mr. Holmes is currently willing to resolve the case to bring the proceedings to a speedy and definite conclusion for all involved," his lawyers wrote in a motion.

This maneuver came only days before the April 1 deadline that newly elected DA George Brauchler had set for making a decision about the death penalty. Prosecutors now said that they were "extremely unlikely" to accept the defense offer—unless Holmes and his lawyers provided "specific access to information that would allow them to fully assess the Defendant and his alleged acts for purposes of determining a just outcome to this case." In other words, the prosecution wanted access to the spiral notebook.

Without that, the plea was unacceptable.

"There is not—and has never been—an actual or unqualified 'offer' to plead guilty," the DA's office wrote in a motion filed by Brauchler himself.

On April 1, the DA did as expected, and with both the victims' relatives and Holmes's parents looking on, he told a jammed courtroom, "It is my determination and my intention that in this case, for James Eagan Holmes, justice is death."

He cited five aggravating circumstances in the theater attack, including the "cruel or depraved" nature of the shootings and the killing of a child. Holmes was now eligible to become the fourth person on Colorado's death row, all of them in the Eighteenth Judicial District (the DA who'd preceded Brauchler in office, Carol Chambers, had been known for favoring capital punishment, and around Denver her nickname among private investigators and defense lawyers was "Death Chambers").

Soon after Brauchler's announcement, the defense broke its silence and wrote in a motion, "Mr. Holmes suffers from a serious mental illness," and may lack a "plausible grounding in reality."

In recent months, he'd twice been transported to a hospital for self-inflicted injuries. Scores of official videos had been taken of him in jail, and some may have captured him trying to hurt himself in his cell, but none had been released to the media or to the public. Was he acting bizarrely in these episodes because he was insane, or was it a performance for the cameras?

Only minutes after Brauchler asked for capital punishment for Holmes, Judge Sylvester surprisingly recused himself from the case and was instantly replaced by the younger and much livelier Judge Carlos Samour. In 1979, Samour had arrived in Colorado as a thirteen-year-old immigrant from El Salvador. He'd graduated from Columbine High School, earned an honors degree in psychology from the University of Colorado-Denver, and then received a law degree from the University of Denver. After spending half a decade in the office of Holland & Hart, he'd accepted a pay cut to become a low-level prosecutor in the Denver District Attorney's office. In 2006, he'd been recommended for a judgeship and had been on the bench ever since.

Judge Sylvester had never looked comfortable presiding over what might have been the most visible and legally entangled prosecution in the state's history. The prosecutors' decision to seek the death penalty, he later explained, meant months of hearings that wouldn't leave enough time for his administrative duties as chief judge of a busy four-county district. Fifteen minutes after he'd stepped aside, Judge Samour took command of the courtroom and was not only fully up to speed on the case, but also was not shy about being inside a large spotlight. Local, regional, national, and occasionally international media had assembled in the courtroom for hearings, with reporters working for news organizations as far away as France and China.

When a journalist covering the case for a Bejing TV station was asked why the Chinese were intrigued by this event, she said, "They're interested in anything that makes America look bad."

Judge Samour spoke casually with the attorneys and gave the impression of a law professor addressing, or correcting, his students. He regularly interrupted legal arguments to help him understand what point the lawyer was trying to make or what issue needed to be clarified. The new judge would not just be an observer in determining

Holmes's legal sanity or insanity; he would play a significant role in how the question was resolved in court.

If Brauchler had not sought the death penalty, the defendant could have pled guilty and received a life sentence, as in the case of mass murderer Jared Loughner. On January 8, 2011, he'd shot and killed six people in Tuscon, Arizona; his primary target had been U.S. Representative Gabrielle Giffords, who was severely injured but survived the attack. Following the shootings, Loughner received treatment until the legal system viewed him as "mentally competent," meaning that he was aware of what was happening in court and able to assist his defense attorneys. He entered his guilty plea, and the case came to what many people regarded as a reasonable conclusion.

In seeking the death penalty against Holmes, Brauchler ensured that the defense lawyers would now use every possible argument and every conceivable legal tool to save the life of their client.

"If I were a victim of this crime or a relative of mine had died or been wounded during the shootings," said an observer in the gallery following the capital punishment announcement, "I would not have closure just because Holmes might eventually be executed. I'd still want to know as much as I could about why he did this. I'd expect the system to at least help me answer that question.

"I'd want to know everything about the available evidence, starting with his notebook and his psychiatric reports from when he was in therapy at Anschutz. Knowing what motivated him is the only thing that would give me some peace, no matter what the answer turned out to be."

If Holmes decided to enter a not guilty by reason of insanity plea, the defense was already balking at having him submit to a polygraph test or to a "narco-analytic interview," in which he'd be given "truth serum" during a mental health exam. The exam was unconstitutional, the defense claimed, because under the influence of the serum he might involuntarily provide information to psychiatrists that would violate his Fifth Amendment guarantee of protection against self-incrimination.

The prosecution dismissed this argument, saying there was no other way to evaluate Holmes's state of mind, except by having him undergo independent testing by a qualified Colorado psychiatrist.

Back and forth the lawyers went, with nothing settled.

Public Defender Daniel King confided to Judge Samour that Holmes had been privately examined by Chicago-based psychologist Robert Hanlon, and the defense was satisfied with what they'd learned. King could "in good faith tender that Mr. Holmes was not guilty by reason of insanity . . . We now have a diagnosis. We now have an opinion by qualified professionals."

The not guilty by reason of insanity plea is used in only about 1 percent of all felony cases nationwide and is successful in roughly one-fourth of them. A person who's legally insane is "incapable of distinguishing right from wrong" at the time of the crime. This is a courtroom definition, not a mental health one. As Dr. Neil Gowensmith of the University of Denver's Forensic Institute for Research Service and Training told *The Denver Post*, "The inability to distinguish right from wrong—that's not in any clinical definition anywhere for any mental disease or disorder . . . Most people with a mental illness or symptoms know right from wrong in the legal sense."

One benchmark of knowing the difference between right and wrong occurs when an offender tries to escape the scene of the crime. Interestingly, Holmes made no attempt to do this.

In June 2013, his defense team officially entered a plea of not guilty by reason of insanity on his behalf, and the judge accepted it, ruling that the state's mental health exam was in fact constitutional. If Holmes were found insane after this exam, he'd likely spend the rest of his life in a mental hospital (although the average stay in a Colorado hospital for homicide is seven and a half years). If he were found sane, he'd stand trial for multiple murders. In early June, the case files—holding 51,000 pages of material and hundreds of CDs and

DVDs—were sent to the Colorado Mental Health Institute at Pueblo, where the psychiatric exam would take place. Judge Samour stipulated that no one at CMHIP could perform a narco-analytic interview with the defendant without first obtaining his permission.

Days before the files were sent off, a twenty-four-year-old Southern California man with a semiautomatic rifle killed four people and wounded five others during a rampage across several blocks of suburban Los Angeles—before police shot him dead in the Santa Monica College Library. For the massacre, John Samir Zawahri, who had a history of mental problems, had worn all black clothing and a load-bearing vest. Like Holmes, he was armed with an AR-15 assault rifle and had the capacity to fire 1,300 rounds of ammunition.

■ ■ ■

Judge Samour also ruled that the spiral notebook could at last become part of the case—since Holmes had, with his plea, relinquished his right to doctor-patient confidentiality and other protections. The Colorado Mental Health Institute appointed Dr. Jeffrey Metzner, a psychiatrist who'd taught at the University of Colorado and consulted with the Institute since 1979, to perform the exam. With Dr. Metzner in place, the defense made a final effort to keep the notebook out of the hands of the psychiatrist and the prosecution, with Daniel King asserting that because the package had been mailed to Dr. Fenton on July 19, just hours before the massacre, but she'd never actually *read* its contents, the notebook wasn't part of their psychiatric relationship.

"Mr. King's argument was a creative one," said Judge Samour, when making his ruling, "but I'm not persuaded by it."

Samour handed over the notebook to Dr. Metzner, and it was officially opened for the first time. Would the pages reveal what had happened to the defendant after he'd moved to Aurora? And what had changed between the winter of 2012—when he was successfully conducting research on the sixth floor of the neuroscience building—and the late spring and early summer of that year? Would the notebook reflect why he'd taken on the persona of The Joker and document his slide into insanity or show the intricate designs of a premeditated killer? Or was it possible that the notebook would demonstrate something more complicated, challenging the very definitions of insanity and mental illness?

Could one be fully functional in society and insane at the same time? Could one move in and out of sanity from one moment to the next? Would the notebook finally provide some answers?

On April 1, 2013, Judge Samour set early February 2014 for the opening of the Holmes trial—a full ten months away. If that seemed like forever to the living victims and their relatives, at least the process was no longer stuck and going nowhere.

Or was it?

XXIII

On June 3, 2013, President Obama gave a major speech about mental illness in the United States. Within a few weeks, Salon would reprint an AlterNet article by Bruce Levine that gave an overview of mental health in America. Some of the findings included:

> A 2001–03 survey of adults conducted by the National Institute of Mental Health found that at some point in their lives "46 percent of Americans met the criteria established by the American Psychiatric Association for at least one mental illness."

> In 1998, Martin Seligman, then president of the American Psychological Association, told the National Press Club that there is now between ten and twenty times as much depression in the United States as there was fifty years ago. Three decades earlier, he said, the average age of the onset of depression was twenty-nine and a half years. Now it's between ages fourteen and fifteen.

> A 2007 *New York Times* report revealed that between 1994 and 2003, treatment for bipolar disorder in American children increased fortyfold. Four years later, the U.S. Centers for Disease Control and Prevention noted a 400 percent increase in national antidepressant usage since 1990, making it the most heavily prescribed drug for Americans eighteen to forty-four. Among women forty to fifty-nine,

23 percent were on antidepressants. The CDC also reported in May 2013 that 13–20 percent of American children experience a mental disorder in a given year.

About a third of the population with a mental illness that should have been in treatment was not because of budget cuts since the start of the 2008 recession—or because they believed that getting help was ineffective or unnecessary. Another 35 percent shunned therapy, afraid that their employers, friends, or families would look down on them for doing so.

In his June 2013 speech, President Obama addressed this issue: "We want to let people living with mental health challenges know that they are not alone and we've got to be making sure that we're committed to supporting those fellow Americans. Because struggling with a mental illness, or caring for someone who does, can be isolating . . . It begins to feel as if, not only are you alone, but that you shouldn't burden others with the challenge. And the darkness, day in, day out—what some call a cloud you just can't seem to escape—begins to close in . . ."

■ ■ ■

On July 9, 2013, Holmes's attorneys admitted in court papers for the first time that the accused was in fact the shooter at the Aurora theater. They reiterated that he suffered from a "severe mental illness" and was "in the throes of a psychotic episode" at the time of the massacre. They also chastised the judge for ruling that if the case went to trial, Holmes would be chained to the floor. Their client had "never once presented as anything other than compliant and well-behaved" in court and Samour's order was "incorrect, troubling, and inhumane."

"The defense's contention," the judge fired back, "while high on rhetoric, is low on substance, as it grossly and unfairly mischaracterizes the Court's ruling . . . The Court chose the least restrictive form of restraint available and the one that could be hidden from the jury's view."

If it was unclear how those examining Holmes in Pueblo would view his drug and alcohol usage in the months prior to the crime, something else was perfectly clear: the vast increase in the intake of prescribed narcotics across the United States in the past few decades—and the effects of this on the general population.

"There are beneficial uses for psychotropic drugs, but the over-utilization of them needs to be put in check," says Don Mares, former President of Mental Health America in Colorado. "We're not in the camp that sees these drugs as being evil. They save lives, but you need a good marriage between drugs and therapy to make things work. There are economic reasons for all this drug use. The psychiatric profession is generally not seen as a top tier medical practice, in economic terms, so that puts pressure on the psychiatric profession. They have the same loans and bills as everyone else in the medical profession and they can make more money in a ten-minute session of prescribing drugs than in talking with someone for an hour, so that's what happens."

Some physicians were pushing back against this trend.

"OxyContin is the heroin pill of our time," says Dr. Ivor Garlick, an internist and addiction specialist who's worked with prison inmates and others to free themselves from prescription drugs. "People use it like heroin—grinding it up and snorting it. There are now more deaths in the country because of the misuse of legal drugs than for overdoses of heroin and cocaine combined.

"After minor surgeries now, doctors might give you about sixty Vicodin and forty Percocet and forty Dilantin. It only takes many people about three weeks to become addicts. There's a lot of pressure on us—from society, the media, and the pharmaceutical companies—to give people these drugs. The pharmaceutical companies spend billions advertising them on TV and have to earn that money back. Patients have come to expect that they'll be given drugs and that they can live without any pain. It isn't realistic. To have no pain is to be unconscious.

"I've lost patients because I won't prescribe them these drugs. After I've refused, they've called me on the phone begging for them. They've called me cruel, but that's all right. I still won't do it. I care about them and about their vulnerability to addiction. I'm trying to break the cycle of abuse and to teach them that these drugs just keep them from learning how to cope with life.

"Narcotics can put you into a hyper-algesiac state, meaning that one has a heightened sensitivity to pain. People take the drugs and that increases the pain receptors in the brain. Let's say you started with ten receptors. On the drug, that number goes up to one hundred. The drug lasts four to six hours and then it wears off, but you still have those one hundred receptors that have been stimulated by the drug. Those receptors are crying out for relief now, and that translates into more pain, so the drug itself is responsible for increasing the pain.

"A big part of this problem is financial, both for pharmaceutical companies and the medical community. Psychiatrists aren't reimbursed for therapy sessions, but they are reimbursed for handing out drugs. So they treat people with medication. Neuroscientists support all this through their research into the brain. They know exactly how to stimulate the brain to get the effects they want, but the basic humanity of the healing process is lost along the way."

■ ■ ■

The message was the same everywhere: drugs and other forms of escape masked the realities that people had trouble living with—and many had no strategy for coping without the escape. There was an endless variety of narcotics one could take to try to dull the pain, for a while, but where were the alternatives for confronting the pain in a more conscious way, rather than simply denying the feelings? These weren't political or social issues, per se. They were emotional and psychological issues, and a reflection of the underlying emotional changes in the culture during the past few decades. The overuse or overprescription of drugs was spelling out that change and making it obvious: People were having greater difficulty adjusting to daily life. If you were a "normal" person, it was more of a struggle. If you were "at risk," how big was the challenge to stay in control of yourself?

One thing we learned from speaking with our son and other millennials was that the world we'd grown up in was gone and wasn't coming back. Some things we'd taken for granted had disappeared for good. Their reality seemed less solid, at deeply personal levels, than the one we'd known in our youth. That meant that one was under a bigger burden to find one's own identity and sense of self.

The conversation around mass shootings was generally focused on gun control, which was clearly an important subject. Guns might be called the hardware of this equation of violence. Emotions were the software—and just as important when deciding whether or not to pick up a firearm.

XXIV

In midsummer 2013, the first anniversary of the Aurora massacre approached. On Friday, July 19, the Mayors Against Illegal Guns (MAIG) campaign, launched in 2006 by New York Mayor Michael Bloomberg and Boston Mayor Thomas Menino, came to the Denver suburbs. Bloomberg, who'd been out in front of this issue for years and would stay there after leaving office in 2014, had personally spent $3 million to back the MAIG coalition. It entailed nearly one thousand mayors nationwide and supported "commonsense reforms" for gun control, including outlawing semiautomatic rifles and standard capacity magazines (which have the ability to hold more than ten rounds). The campaign itself was represented by a long, shiny, black recreational vehicle called "The National Drive to Reduce Gun Violence," which showed up at gun control rallies around the country. The RV's side held a few names of those Americans recently killed by firearms and on this Friday morning, it was parked at Aurora's Cherry Creek State Park.

Attending the event were Tom Sullivan, the father of twenty-seven-year-old Alex, killed in Theater Nine; Coni Sanders, whose father Dave was a teacher at Columbine in 1999 and was murdered while saving others at the school; Jane Dougherty, whose sister Mary Sherlach had been a psychologist at Sandy Hook Elementary School before being gunned down in the Newtown shooting; and Carlee Soto, whose sister Victoria, a teacher at Sandy Hook, was also slain there.

At noon, the Aurora event commenced with twenty-three-year-old Stephen Barton, a survivor of the theater shooting and a MAIG associate, delivering a memorial for gun victims everywhere. In December 2012, Barton was at home in Connecticut and recovering from his recent wounds when Adam Lanza opened fire at Sandy Hook Elementary, about ten miles from where Barton lived.

While he spoke to those gathered at the park, a dozen members of Gun Rights Across America and Rocky Mountain Gun Owners stood across the parking lot from the MAIG event, protesting and waving signs touting the Second Amendment. One read, "Down With Bloomberg/Hickenlooper Cabal." In between the MAIG group and the protesters were police cars and heavily armed officers.

All Friday afternoon and evening and then deep into the night, MAIG supporters read the names of their 2,500 fellow citizens who'd been murdered by gun violence just since the Newtown shootings seven months earlier (this number excluded suicides and those killed in law enforcement actions). In soft voices that wavered and occasionally cracked, the readers checked off the names of those slain in the first half of 2013. After each name, they said "killed by a gun" and gave the date and location of the crime, laying out a map of bloodshed that spread to every corner of the nation.

On the side of the RV was the address of MAIG's website: www.nomorenames.org.

■ ■ ■

A few hundred yards away, along the waterfront of Cherry Creek Reservoir, gun-rights advocates held their own rally, as children skittered across the sandy beach and speedboats made waves farther out from shore. The temperature was moderate and a light breeze made for a perfect afternoon in a perfectly divided park, with little or no common ground between the two contending groups. The gun control crowd wore T-shirts proclaiming "Moms Demand Action," while the gun-rights advocates donned attire announcing "I Will Not Comply," "Don't Tread on Me," "This is Not a Gun Free Zone," and "Liberty's Teeth" scrawled over the image of a handgun. They wore orange NRA caps and strolled through the park with defiance and wariness, as if expecting to be insulted or attacked.

They hadn't intended to hold their rally today but felt that because MAIG was politicizing the one-year anniversary of the Aurora shootings, they had to make their presence felt. On the park's gravel roads, they drove vintage cars and trucks back and forth past the MAIG event, their vehicles adorned with American flags and sayings from Thomas Jefferson, John Adams, and Tom Paine opposing gun control and the overreach of government.

As July 19 gave way to the 20th, the reading of the victims' names went on and on. At precisely 12:38 a.m., the exact moment Holmes had begun firing a year earlier in Theater Nine, the MAIG supporters stood in the moonlight and read the names of those killed that night:

Jon Blunk
AJ Boik
Jesse Childress
Gordon Cowden
Jessica Redfield Ghawi
John Larimer
Matt McQuinn
Micayla Medek
Veronica Moser-Sullivan
Alex Sullivan
Alex Teves
Rebecca Wingo

In another part of Aurora, people gathered across from Theater Nine and held up candles in the spot where a dozen makeshift crosses had stood in the aftermath of the carnage. Some wore Batman-logo apparel and placed signs and flowers around twelve new crosses installed for this occasion. They formed a large circle, holding hands and praying, as the Aurora police drove by in a line of cruisers with their emergency lights flashing.

Weeks before this evening, Aurora Police Chief Dan Oates and City Manager Skip Noe had sent out a "7/20 One-Year Anniversary" memo to police and municipal workers.

"Studies clearly show," it read, "that anniversaries of this type sometimes bring up unhappy feelings or even unrelated unhappy memories that can cause distress, lack of sleep, unexpected emotions, an inability to focus or function at one's usual level, and more . . . look out for each other and be aware of someone, or even ourselves, who may need some additional support at this time."

Two survivors of the massacre chose to turn the anniversary into a celebration. Twenty-one-year-old Eugene Han and twenty-two-year-old Kristin Davis were childhood friends who'd lived through the tragedy together and decided to get married on July 20, 2013.

That same day, a *Denver Post* editorial stated that Saturday marked the one-year anniversary of an event that had brought the community "anguish it had not felt on such a scale since the shootings at Columbine High School in 1999. Colorado has gone from a state where gun control was a topic so far off the political radar that even few Democrats wanted to talk about it, much less do anything about it, to a state that has enacted reasonable—dare we say modest—firearms restrictions. Where the public and even the governor a year ago had been skeptical of new gun control measures, polling has since shown overwhelming support for limiting high-capacity magazines and enacting background checks for all gun sales, legislation which Colorado lawmakers approved . . ."

"What happened in Aurora," the *Post* had to concede a year later, "got the discussion started."

The scope of what Holmes had done in a minute or two inside the theater was laid out in a *Post* article detailing the financial cost of the shootings twelve months later. The wounded had collectively spent six-hundred-plus days in hospitals, and those medical and mental health facilities had donated more than $4 million to the victims in "charity care"—charging nothing for the immediate treatment they'd received. Holmes's actions had taken over $3 million out of local government and school budgets (this did not include his ongoing Public Defender bill), and private donors had given more than $5 million to help the victims. The City of Aurora had spent $1 million studying the aftermath of the crime, and Cinemark Century Theaters had spent another million to renovate the movie complex, which had lost $3 million in revenue during its six-month closure for repairs.

The University of Colorado had spent in excess of $1 million in legal fees to provide representatives for Dr. Fenton, members of the BETA team, and a campus police officer. The school had spent another $85,000 on public-relations consultants and $52,000 for added security. The extra security costs within the Eighteenth Judicial District for Holmes's courtroom appearances amounted to just under a third of a million dollars.

By July 2013, the overall price of the tragedy was very conservatively estimated at $17 million—and the legal proceedings were just getting started.

From a twenty-four-year-old female grad student in Boston:

It feels like we've been on the brink of real change in our society for quite a while, but it just hasn't come yet. We keep waiting for it to arrive. We keep watching older people fight with each other and get nothing done. Change is what people my age are looking for and what they talk about and what they want to believe in. We need gun control and we need more health care and more mental health care and we need economic change and we need some other basic changes. It's what everyone talks about. It's just common sense. We're ready for that now.

We're done with what doesn't work and with the people who support it. We're at the end of that. It's time for something new.

XXV

At midnight on August 6, 2013, Holmes was shipped out of Arapahoe County and transported 100 miles south to the state hospital in Pueblo. The mental health staff had spent months clearing out a forensic wing of the facility for the psychiatrists to test him in. They were assigned to address three basic questions: Was the defendant sane at the time of the shooting? Was he currently mentally competent to stand trial? Did he suffer from a mental illness that could provide a valid defense against the death penalty? As this process played out in Pueblo, Holmes's lawyers kept up a barrage of motions—scores of them, eventually hundreds of them, piling up week after week designed to prolong or save his life, if he were found sane and then convicted and faced the death penalty.

While they kept the judge busy, the secrecy around the proceedings in Pueblo was impenetrable. Dr. Hal Wortzel, Director of Neuropsychiatry Service at the University of Colorado's School of Medicine, had performed roughly two hundred of these evaluations himself. He agreed to speak about the general protocol at the mental hospital without getting into the specifics of the Holmes case.

"Some people undergoing this kind of exam," says Dr. Wortzel, "will try to fake their mental illness. They'll say they can't remember anything or they'll exaggerate their behavior. This is called 'malingering' and we have paper and pencil tests that try to detect it, but we also have a lot of other data to draw on. Before a psychiatrist or psychiatric team comes in to evaluate a patient staying at the Pueblo facility, that patient will have been under observation 24/7 for some amount of time. If someone has been hallucinating every day throughout the day, or talking to the walls, that behavior will be observed and passed along to those doing the exam. If the patient's sleep is disjointed or if he's neglecting basic personal hygiene, that will also be noted. It's one thing to try to fool a psychiatrist for a couple of hours in a face-to-face situation, but another to try to fool an entire staff for a much longer period of time.

"When I'm doing these kinds of evaluations, I ask the patient very open-ended questions, like: 'Tell me what happened. Help me understand why you did this . . .' While it's more difficult to conduct this exam on someone a year after the events, in the vast majority of cases you can render an opinion about their sanity with a high level of confidence. You aren't working for the DA's office or the defense. You're there to give a fully independent evaluation, and the state just wants you to do your job."

■ ■ ■

On August 21, Holmes was returned to the Arapahoe County jail, and sixteen days later copies of the 128-page report generated on him in Pueblo were given to the prosecution and defense. While the media awaited the revelations surrounding the sanity exam (and perhaps even the contents of the spiral notebook), the defense kept up its legal assault. On September 3 alone, Holmes's lawyers filed twenty-one new motions, most of them protesting capital punishment.

"The death penalty," they wrote, "is in steep and consistent decline in Colorado . . . Even if this Court restricts its view to the Colorado Constitution it should strike the death penalty as inconsistent with the evolving standards of decency that mark the progress of a maturing society."

In a 2013 *Denver Post* editorial, Arapahoe County DA George Brauchler wrote, "Our elected prosecutors prudently exercise discretion as to which few murder cases truly warrant the pursuit of the death penalty. Which killer currently facing death in Colorado deserves a lesser sentence?"

■ ■ ■

Since the Aurora massacre, other members of the defendant's generation had begun appearing in the news again and again, making headlines for their own violent behavior. Following numerous mass shootings in the summer of 2012, the carnage continued into 2013, but with a twist. On April 15, near the finish line of the Boston Marathon, two pressure cooker bombs detonated, killing three people and injuring 264. Days later, the suspects were identified as brothers Tamerlan and Dzhokhar Tsarnaev, ages twenty-six and nineteen. The suspects also allegedly killed an MIT officer, Sean Collier; carjacked an SUV; and traded bullets with the police in Watertown, Massachusetts. During the mayhem, Dzhokhar ran over Tamerlan, who died, but the younger brother escaped and led police on a door-to-door manhunt through suburban Boston. When he was caught, he told authorities that he and Tamerlan were motivated by the American wars in Iraq and Afghanistan. Their actions were a political statement delivered though calculated domestic terrorism.

On Monday morning, September 16, 2013, Aaron Alexis stepped inside Building 197, home to three thousand employees at the Navy Yard complex in Washington, DC. At 8:15 a.m., the thirty-four-year-old naval defense contractor opened fire with a shotgun from a fourth-floor overlook and then a third-floor hallway, spraying bullets into a glass-walled cafeteria as workers ate breakfast. Weeks earlier, he'd informed the police in Newport, Rhode Island, that he heard voices that wanted to harm him and that people were following him and using a microwave machine to feed damaging vibrations into his body. The authorities relayed this information to the Newport Naval Station, but no one there saw Alexis as a threat.

By August 25, he'd left Rhode Island for the DC area, where he worked at the Navy Yard for a defense-related computer company. Living in hotels, he had trouble sleeping and was on the antidepressant Trazodone while undergoing treatment from the Department of Veterans Affairs. None of his actions caused him to lose his security clearance. On Saturday, September 14, he visited the Sharpshooters Small Arms Range in Lorton, Virginia, just southwest of the nation's capital. He bought bullets, rented a rifle, and took target practice, before purchasing a shotgun and twenty-four shells. Two days later, he walked into the Navy Yard—protected by armed guards and metal detectors—carrying his base pass and shotgun. Once inside Building 197, he took a handgun from a security officer and began firing. By the time he'd stopped shooting, nearly half an hour later, eight people were injured, twelve were dead, and the police had killed Alexis himself.

Interlude

If there was little in our culture to counter this bloodshed, there was plenty to buttress the notion that violence *was* the best available answer, starting with video games like *Call of Duty* and the *Grand Theft Auto* (*GTA*) series.

"The point of *GTA*," Eric explained, "is to create chaos and mayhem and to kill as many people as possible. But it isn't just about shooting people. In some of these games, you can fly the same jet that went into the World Trade Center in 2001 into a building in California. There are no limits. You can go on a monster rampage and earn stars for the amount of destruction you create. The more you destroy, the more stars you get."

Like many parents with kids around our son's age, we really didn't know much about these games or how popular they remained for many young men long after they'd left childhood behind. When Eric told us early on that we didn't understand things about his growing up and his continuing process of socialization in American culture, this was part of what he meant.

"When you get five stars in these games," he went on, "it means the Army is coming for you. And that means you're really important. That importance feels good. The truth is that these destructive impulses are inside of young men and it's fun to let them out and to not be a 'civilized' person all the time. Guys in my house at college came home from class and played these games for two or three hours a night. They were studying to be scientists and engineers and their courses were very demanding. This was how they unwound in the evening. It isn't just people my age playing them. Eight-year-old kids are also doing it. And they're seeing that the guy being tortured in the video games has darker skin than the guy doing the torturing.

"The game is reinforcing every racial or religious stereotype out there. When guys play it together, they scream out the most violent, racist, and anti-Muslim stuff imaginable. People my age love what's called extreme humor and they let out extreme slurs all the time: 'niggers, beaners, fags, Arabs, and sand niggers.'

"You worry about how these games affect the mentally ill young men who go out and commit crimes or mass shootings, but what is it doing to my friends and to other so-called normal people? How does it influence them? In these games, my friends blow up all kinds of things and think it's hilarious. But when somebody actually does something like this, it's the worst thing that ever happened.

"Each generation of *Grand Theft Auto* has been made to be more realistic. The blood and the gore now look totally real. We're talking about graphic images of torn flesh and ripped muscles. These video game companies have pumped thousands, if not millions, of dollars into research to make the violent details more realistic. And they've succeeded.

"There isn't a draft anymore, but there is a kind of psychological preparation for recruiting young men into the military. Some of the kids joining the armed forces today are the kids that have been playing these video games since they were very young. You train people through these games and through military movies to become soldiers, but not all of them are going to join the army. Some of them see the enemy as not the people in the Middle East, but as the other kids inside their school or somewhere else in America. You can't control everything you create."

As Eric and others have pointed out, the "surgical strikes" of the drone warfare that the U.S. military has used in various parts of the world during the Obama presidency conjure up nothing so much as a video game. According to drone pilot Lt. Col. Matt Martin in his book *Predator*, operating a drone is "almost like playing the computer game *Civilization*." The military terminology for a person killed in a drone strike is "bug splat."

Drone strikes and mass shootings have one other thing in common: the victims are usually indiscriminate.

■ ■ ■

In late summer 2013, Rockstar North brought out *Grand Theft Auto V* (*GTA V*), the most successful launch in entertainment history. During the next three days, consumers bought $800 million worth of the product, and then pushed the number past a billion. In the game, the character Trevor is ordered by the FIB (read: FBI) to extract information from an Azerbaijani fugitive to get the location, identity, and description of an assassination target considered dangerous by the authorities. Trevor, along with the person who's interactively playing the game with him, uses waterboarding and other forms of torture to get that information—even when it's unproductive. As soon as *GTA V* was introduced, the game was compared to the tactics used by the United States over the past decade in America's "War on Terror."

Trevor says to the fugitive, "The media and the government would have us believe that torture is some necessary thing. We need it to get information, to assert ourselves. Did we get any information out of you?"

"I would have told you everything!" the man replies.

"Exactly!" Trevor tells him. "Torture's for the torturer. Or the guy giving the order to the torturer. You torture for the good times! We should all admit that. It's useless as a means of getting information."

A few critics who had accepted the earlier versions of the game felt that *GTA V* had finally gone too far.

Keith Best, chief executive of the group Freedom from Torture, told *The Guardian*, "Rockstar North has crossed a line by effectively forcing people to take on the role of a torturer and perform a series of unspeakable acts if they want to achieve success in the game. Torture is a reality, not a game, and glamourizing it in popular culture undoes the work of organizations like Freedom from Torture and survivor activists to campaign against it. This adds insult to injury for survivors who are left physically and mentally scarred by torture in the real world."

On August 12, 2014, the *Huffington Post* reported that the widely popular *Grand Theft Auto* video game series "lets players get away with a wide range of virtual crimes, including looting and murder. But that's not enough mayhem for some players, who are rewriting its code to add another crime: rape."

Coming video game attractions in 2015 were *Body Count* and *Hatred*, featuring, among other things, a mass murder villain who begins a "genocide crusade" to kill innocent civilians and police officers.

■ ■ ■

Dr. Larry Wahlberg is a clinical psychologist and program manager for the PTSD Residential Rehabilitation Treatment program at a Denver V.A. hospital. He treats both retired military personnel and those still on active duty.

"There are two major types of memory and learning," he says. "One type is Deductive Learning that comes from memory: You learn that Denver is the capital of Colorado by repeating this again and again. The second type is called Procedural Learning and it comes from repetitive actions and practice, like shooting a basketball over and over until you become good at it. One of the problems with video games is that you're learning to kill repetitively in simulated situations. You get better at it and you get more desensitized to the process.

"This is the same purpose that you find in basic training in the military. You repeatedly put young people in situations where they'd normally freeze up or think twice before acting. You put them in these dangerous situations over and over until their reactions become automatic. You condition them until their resistance to committing violence lessens, and then until it's gone.

"Back in the twentieth century, large numbers of soldiers didn't want to shoot at targets in combat. The Army seized upon new principles of learning theory, like behavior modification, in order to overcome this resistance. They used videos to have soldiers repetitively practice shooting at more and more realistic-looking human targets.

"With the new video technologies, you can make things astonishingly realistic. The goal is to help the soldiers achieve mastery over their experience in combat. It's to lessen their anxiety in those situations and to lessen their avoidance of trauma-related stimuli. This in turn will lessen the emotional impact on them for doing their job. Under these circumstances, people see the violence they're creating as an act of justice. They think they're doing the right thing."

In her upcoming book *Mind Change: How Digital Technologies Are Leaving Their Mark on Our Brains*, Oxford-trained neurologist Susan Greenfield writes about how scientists have recorded the brain activity of experienced video gamers who played an average of fourteen hours per week: "Results showed that areas of the brain linked with emotion and empathy (the cingulate cortex and the amygdala) were less active during violent video gaming . . . These areas must be suppressed during violent video gaming, just as they would be in real life, in order to act violently without hesitation."

A HOUSE DIVIDED

XXVI

In the fall of 2013, as the defense team and prosecution lawyers squabbled in front of Judge Samour, the American government shut down due to internal conflict between the two major political parties. On October 1, 2013, 800,000 federal workers were furloughed because Congress and President Obama could not agree on a bill to fund the country's public business. Two days later, a thirty-four-year-old dental hygienist named Miriam Carey was shot to death outside the U.S. Capitol after she tried to ram her car through a White House barrier. The car also held her one-year-old daughter, Erica, who was unharmed. Carey had led police on a chase down Constitution Avenue to the Capitol, which caused a brief lockdown of Congress.

Like Aaron Alexis, Carey suffered from delusions, believing that President Obama was communicating with her. Nearly a year earlier, she'd undergone a mental health evaluation after an encounter with Stamford, Connecticut, police, telling them that she was a prophet, that President Obama would place Stamford under a "lockdown," and that her residence was under electronic surveillance.

The day after her death, a sixty-four-year-old New Jersey man, John Constantino, set himself on fire with gasoline on the National Mall in Washington, DC. As he burned, nearby joggers took off their shirts to try to douse the flames. No motive was known for this act of self-immolation, and he died the next morning.

. . .

While awaiting the results of Holmes's sanity exam, the defense team tried to decrease the flow of information even further, asking the judge to stop posting legal motions on the Arapahoe County website. The defense efforts would eventually lead them to petition the U.S. Supreme Court to find out who'd leaked the contents of the spiral notebook to Fox reporter Jana Winter—still the only person, outside of a few medical personnel, to have knowledge of the notebook's contents. (The justices later ruled in favor of Winter). The move to take the postings off the website prompted a national organization of journalists, the Reporters Committee for Freedom of the Press, to launch a protest with Judge Samour. The RCFP board included Wolf Blitzer of CNN, Andrea Mitchell of NBC News, and Michael Duffy of *Time* magazine, all supporting the Colorado Press Association and the Colorado Freedom of Information Coalition in their efforts to defeat the defense request. The combined groups wrote a letter to the judge, which illuminated critical issues not just in this case, but facing the entire country.

"The defendant's motion," they wrote, "asks the court to 1) suppress all transcripts of the proceedings, 2) suppress the register of actions, and 3) remove access to most pleadings from its website . . . We write to encourage this court to understand the broader implications of the defendant's position . . .

"These actions would significantly burden the public's understanding of issues of national importance . . . The public interest at stake here is profound. This case and other recent mass shootings have prompted nationwide debate and dialog on a wide range of issues involving violence and mental health: the necessity of requiring mental health background checks before gun purchases; the efficacy of mental health treatment in this country; the role of universities in addressing psychiatric issues of students; and the effects of violence in popular culture . . .

"At a vigil in Newtown, Connecticut, following the shootings at Sandy Hook Elementary School, President Obama cited the Aurora case before calling for reform, announcing that 'I will use whatever power this office holds to engage my fellow citizens—from law enforcement to mental health professionals to parents and educators—in an effort aimed at preventing more tragedies like this . . .'

"Following that speech, President Obama announced that Vice President Joe Biden would lead an effort to develop policy proposals aimed at reducing gun violence. After the killings at the Navy Yard in Washington, DC, President Obama again named Aurora before stressing the need for both restrictions on guns and reform in mental health care, stating: 'As a society, it's clear we've got to do a better job of ensuring that those who need mental health care actually get it, and that in those efforts, we don't stigmatize those who need help . . .'

"These issues are not just local, but national in scope. This court has a constitutional obligation to let members of the public see all the evidence so that they can make informed decisions regarding these important policy debates . . . The Supreme Court has repeatedly found that excessive secrecy in criminal trials limits truthful reporting on matters of public concern, and therefore implicates First Amendment values . . ."

The letter concluded:

"Importantly, in this case, defense attorneys are primarily concerned with whether he [Holmes] qualifies for the insanity defense. This makes it even more important that the public learns about the mental health issues in this case. If the defendant is found not responsible due to insanity, an informed public would more likely trust that the judicial process was fair . . ."

■ ■ ■

On November 1, 2013, U.S. Attorney General Eric Holder said at the annual conference of the International Association of Chiefs of Police that the average number of mass shooting incidents had tripled in recent years. From 2000 to 2008, the United States had experienced an average of five such shootings each year, with a total of 324 people shot and 145 killed. From 2009 to 2012, 404 people were shot and 207 were killed. In 2013 to date, Holder said, there had been at least a dozen such massacres. During the past decade, the Justice Department had trained fifty thousand front-line officers, along with more than seven thousand on-scene commanders and three thousand local, state, and federal agency heads to respond to active shooters. Every day, the FBI's Behavioral Threat Assessment Center worked with local police and other law enforcement personnel to assess people who might become violent.

After years of stalling and denial, mass shootings had at last become a national priority.

As the Attorney General was speaking at the conference, a young man carrying anti-government material and an AR-15 assault rifle, like the one Holmes had used, walked into Los Angeles International Airport and opened fire, blasting his way through security at Terminal 3, killing one Transportation Security Administration worker and wounding seven others. Before leaving for the airport that morning, he'd sent a suicidal text message to his family.

The gunman, twenty-three-year-old Paul Anthony Ciancia, was wounded by law enforcement and taken to a hospital in critical condition. His anti-government views had motivated him to murder the TSA employee and to think about killing himself.

A witness at the airport reported that the shooter had calmly entered and strolled through the terminal flashing his weapon, approaching him with a one-word question: "TSA?"

When the answer was no, Ciancia kept walking until he found the employee he was searching for.

A second TSA worker was shot in the leg, and other bystanders were treated for lesser injuries.

■ ■ ■

On November 8, nearly sixteen months into the case, the silence surrounding Holmes's sanity exam finally began to break apart when the defense lawyers indicated in a motion that the evaluation had shown the defendant to be too mentally ill to face capital punishment. They asked the judge to throw out the death penalty "because the state and federal constitutions prohibit the execution of individuals such as Mr. Holmes who suffer from a chronic and serious mental illness." A second defense motion requested that Judge Samour prevent the prosecution from bringing into the trial statements Holmes had made during the exam. A third motion requested that the judge "exclude evidence and findings concerning competency to stand trial." They'd continue this barrage for months and years to come.

Prosecutors openly disagreed with one of the sanity report findings and asked the court to order Holmes to undergo further mental health testing by *their own* experts. Local defense attorney Dan Recht told *The Denver Post* that this request was "a clear indication that the prosecution is unhappy with the state hospital evaluation. It certainly suggests that the opinion of the state hospital psychiatrists is favorable to the Holmes defense of insanity."

Holmes's legal team opposed a new evaluation, and Judge Samour took the matter under consideration, unleashing a new round of questions. If the psychiatrists in Pueblo had indeed found Holmes insane, would DA Brauchler go forward and try him at enormous effort and cost? Or would he drop the death penalty and agree to put Holmes in prison or a mental hospital possibly for life? If Holmes was insane, was there any reason for the legal case to proceed? If it ended now, would the press and public ever know what the psychiatrists had actually concluded about Holmes in the summer of 2013—or learn the contents of the spiral notebook?

The longer the case went on, the less it revealed about Holmes and the more it revealed about the lack of common ground within a legal system charged with dealing with the shooter's actions. The dysfunction inside that system seemed to be matched by the relentless violence that continued to unfold outside of it.

On November 21, to the dismay of the victims, their kin, and many others, Judge Samour once again delayed the upcoming trial, previously scheduled to start in early February 2014. Samour set a hearing on the sanity issue for mid-December 2013.

"I want to give every motion as much attention as they deserve," he said. "I've been working night and day and weekends . . . My life is on hold."

The defense filed a motion to bar the media, the public, and the victims from this critical December proceeding, which would include the testimony of Dr. Jeffrey Metzner, the chief psychiatrist who specialized in the mental health of prison inmates and who'd examined Holmes in Pueblo. *The Denver Post* had already written that the level of secrecy surrounding the case had become "absurd," and now other media outlets, including *The New York Times*, *Los Angeles Times*, CBS News, CNN, and National Public Radio, joined the chorus of protest, petitioning Judge Samour to be allowed into the hearing.

"The public," the collective media wrote in its motion, "has a profound and, indeed, compelling interest in monitoring the conduct of the judicial branch of government and the criminal justice process, particularly in capital punishment cases such as this one, in which so many people's lives were cut short, and others' forever transformed, by the Defendant's admitted conduct."

While this motion was being considered, University of New Haven student William Dong's Facebook cover photo featured Heath Ledger portraying The Joker in *The Dark Knight*. In December 2013, the twenty-two-year-old Fairfield, Connecticut, resident was arraigned on multiple gun-related charges after being arrested near the UNH campus. When taken into custody, he was carrying two Glock hand-guns, a Bushmaster AR-15 assault-style rifle, and newspaper clippings about the shootings in Aurora. His Facebook profile "liked" pages for Glock, IGun Pro, and several video games, including *Gears of War, Saints Row Rage,* and *Call of Duty.*

■ ■ ■

Friday, the 13th of December, was one day before the first anniversary of the massacre at Sandy Hook Elementary School in Newtown, Connecticut. That afternoon Judge Samour decided to postpone the sanity hearing until the end of January 2014.

As Samour was making his ruling, eighteen-year-old Karl Pierson, a senior at Arapahoe High in suburban Denver, walked into his 2,100-student school carrying a cache of weapons. The school was just a few miles away from Columbine High. And it would later be discovered that Pierson strongly identified with Columbine shooter, Eric Harris. Pierson had a pump-action shotgun, three incendiary devices in his backpack, and a machete concealed in a scabbard. He had two bandoliers of ammunition, holding more than 125 rounds, strapped to his chest and waist. Scrawled on his arm were letters and numbers associated with five classrooms and the school's library. Inside his forearm was the Latin phrase *Alea iacta est,* meaning "the die has been cast," a line attributed to Julius Caesar while crossing the Rubicon River with his troops to start a civil war.

Three months earlier, Pierson had threatened to kill his debate teacher, Tracy Murphy. A gifted debater, Pierson had strong political opinions, and earlier in the school year had been removed by Murphy as the captain of the debate team and then suspended. Following the suspension, the school psychologist spoke with Pierson but decided that he was a "low level of concern." Pierson's mother took him to a mental health center, where therapists determined he wasn't dangerous. Pierson had shown some of his fellow students images of the gun and machete he'd bought but didn't tell them about his upcoming plans.

After Murphy told school officials that he was afraid for his life, they didn't suspend Pierson, but his mother made him stay home from school for three days. According to an Arapahoe County Sheriff's report published months after the shooting, Pierson said he wanted to kill Murphy, and this was captured on a parking lot video, but the tape was erased before anyone acted on it.

On December 13, when he came across his fellow students in the hallway, Pierson demanded they tell him where he could find Murphy. They didn't. When Murphy learned that Pierson was stalking him, he was hustled out of the building to safety, but not before Pierson aimed two shots at him and missed. Frustrated at not being able to locate his target, Pierson fired his shotgun five times down a hallway, hitting a student in the face and saying between shots, "Where's Murphy? Where's Murphy? Where's Murphy?"

He ignited a Molotov cocktail, using it to set fire to three bookshelves in the library.

One of the shotgun blasts critically injured a seventeen-year-old female student, Claire Esther Davis, who was taken to a hospital in a coma (with people across Denver praying for her, she died a week later).

As a sheriff's deputy closed in on him in the hallways, Pierson went into a classroom and killed himself. Friends and acquaintances of the Pierson family later described the young man as a very dedicated and bright student who came from a religious family that regularly attended Bible study.

Three months before the shooting, Pierson wrote in his diary that he'd bought a gun and "mom does not know about it . . . I will shoot up my school, Arapahoe high school, before the year is over . . . I am a psychopath with a superiority complex . . . I will do something I have wanted to do for a while—mass murder and be in a place of power where I and I alone are judge, jury, and executioner."

Following his rampage, he wrote, he hoped that people would talk about "elementary school teasing . . . Words hurt, can mold a socio-path, and will lead someone a decade later to kill."

On the day of the shooting, Pierson went bowling and bought Mountain Dew in order to use the glass bottles for Molotov cocktails.

"Today is going to be fun," he wrote in his diary.

From a twenty-five-year-old male working on his master's in computer science in Chicago:

> It isn't just one thing that's creating the mass shooting phenomenon. For some kids bulling begins on the first day they enter school and doesn't stop. Plus all the competition. Plus the pressure to succeed and make a lot of money.
>
> Every day I live in fear that someone on my campus will pick up a gun and explode into violence. Every time I enter a classroom, I think about it. What happens if an active shooter walks in the door? The school sends out e-mails about ADAPT (Adolescent, Development, and Preventative Treatment). I get these e-mails four times a year. Older people didn't grow up with that fear, but those my age haven't had any choice about it. It's right in our faces every week or every day. Nothing in our culture teaches us how to deal with trauma.

XXVII

In early 2014, the Washington, DC–based American Psychological Association released its first-ever survey about teenagers called "Stress in America." It found that more than a quarter (27 percent) of U.S. teenagers said they experience "extreme stress" during the school year, as compared to only 13 percent during the summer months. The one thousand teens interviewed reported that high stress levels were negatively affecting every part of their lives, putting them at risk for many physical and emotional ills, and perhaps even shorter lifespans. Forty percent of them felt irritable or angry, while one-third said they were overwhelmed, depressed, or sad.

"Our study . . . gives us a window in looking at how early these patterns might begin," the Association's CEO and clinical psychologist Norman Anderson told *USA Today*. "The patterns of stress we see in adults seem to be occurring as early as the adolescent years—stress-related behaviors such as lack of sleep, lack of exercise, poor eating habits . . ."

A few people looked at these numbers and did not draw the predictable conclusions.

"Depression is very common in our society, and the evolution of depression is a very interesting thing," says Denver psycho-pharmacologist Jeffrey Gold. "Some disorders gradually phase out of the population and the number of cases gets smaller, but not with depression.

It stays about the same over time. If it's so bad for us, why wouldn't it become less prevalent? One theory is that there is an evolutionary *benefit* to depression. That means that if you're not getting the outcomes you want, your brain tells you to change. Depression is an adaptive function to those conditions. The brain is saying, 'Change something in your behavior.' If you take a drug for depression, the drug is telling you, 'Ignore the message from your brain. Avoid the discomfort.'

"We're looking at this as if the brain isn't working properly, but what if it's doing exactly what it's supposed to be doing and we're not paying attention to that? We're trying to eliminate feelings that are there for a good reason and we're ignoring the adaptive mechanism. In the patient's mind, this creates an illusion about what it means to be human and what kinds of feelings and experiences one can expect. It denies what we are. Maybe what people feel is exactly what they should be feeling."

Then he added with emphasis, "Maybe teaching them better coping skills is exactly what we should be focusing on, not taking more drugs."

■ ■ ■

A 2012 study in the journal *Clinical Psychological Science* found that rates of suicide attempts were significantly higher in adolescents ages thirteen to seventeen than in emerging adults (ages eighteen to twenty-three) or adults (twenty-four to thirty). In the past decade, America's overall suicide rate had risen 15 percent and had become the leading cause of injury-related death, surpassing combat deaths in the U.S. military.

The accumulation of data was finally breaking apart the indifference or inaction around the issue of mass murder in America. Three days before Pierson's attack inside Arapahoe High, Vice President Joe Biden had announced that $100 million would be sent to community mental health centers across the country to provide more access to care—in part to prevent suicides.

The White House then put forth two new executive actions increasing the federal background-check system. The first expanded the definition of the term "committed to a mental institution" to include persons incompetent to stand trial or not guilty by reason of mental disease or defect; persons lacking mental responsibility or deemed insane; and persons found guilty but mentally ill, regardless of whether these determinations are made by a state, local, federal, or military court.

"We are taking an important, commonsense step to clarify the federal firearms regulations, which will strengthen our ability to keep dangerous weapons out of the wrong hands," Attorney General Eric Holder said in a statement. "This step will provide clear guidance on who is prohibited from possessing firearms under federal law for reasons related to mental health . . ."

The second proposed rule change allowed certain entities that were covered by patient privacy protections to submit additional information to the background-check system. "There is a strong public safety need for this information to be accessible to the [National Instant Criminal Background Check System], and some states are currently under-reporting or not reporting certain information to the NICS at all," Health and Human Services Secretary Kathleen Sebelius said in a statement. "This proposed rulemaking is carefully balanced to protect and preserve individuals' privacy interests, the patient-provider relationship, and the public's health and safety."

■ ■ ■

On December 20, 2013, seventeen months after the Aurora massacre, Judge Samour ruled that the late January 2014 sanity hearing would be closed to the media, the public, and to the victims and their relatives. No transcript of the proceedings would be available to anyone but the judge and lawyers. The hearing, expected to last as long as a week, would reveal some of Dr. Metzner's work with Holmes in Pueblo and some of what he'd concluded about the defendant's mental state during the shootings. It might even reveal a part of what was in the spiral notebook, but no one outside the legal system would have access to any of this information.

In his ruling, the judge mentioned the prosecution's claim that the exam of Holmes had been faulty because Metzner "had an unfair bias." Prosecutors had challenged two of Metzner's conclusions, one related to Holmes's sanity at the time of the shootings and the other regarding whether he was mentally fit to be eligible for the death penalty following his trial. The prosecution wanted to draw its own conclusions about these matters through further testing by a pair of its own experts. The defense was adamantly opposed to a second exam. Both sides argued their case at the January hearing and put their psychiatric experts on display, but the public and the media were kept away from all such discussions.

Never had lawyers worked so hard to keep the general population from learning anything about the mind or the emotions of a mass killer. Never had it been more difficult to get beneath the façade of a crime in which nearly every pertinent physical fact was already known and there was no question of guilt and innocence: James Holmes was the shooter. Never had the public interest been greater, because the American populace not only paid for the legal system, and was not only called upon to serve on juries, but it kept getting terrorized and maimed and murdered by those with significant mental health issues.

The only thing louder than the silence coming out of the Eighteenth Judicial District and the Arapahoe County Courthouse was the ongoing violence being perpetrated by people from Holmes's generation.

"You can learn almost nothing relevant in the field of psychiatry now because everything is kept confidential," says Denver therapist and author Joycee Kennedy, who was a first responder at Columbine. "It's a complete travesty. This is why there's so little accurate information about patients and so few accurate diagnoses. It's why the mental health field isn't making the progress we should be making. We have the right to know what psychological and emotional processes created James Holmes.

"I was on emergency call at Aurora Mental Health Center one day a week for five years, which meant that I evaluated any Aurora resident taken to jail or to an area hospital. It would take a professional less than one minute to diagnose James Holmes as having a serious mental disorder. When someone gets to the point of making homicidal threats and buying guns and a gas mask and identifying himself as The Joker, his brain has gone offline.

"The insanity plea everyone is fighting over in this case is meaningless and archaic. It doesn't matter whether he was willful or not at the time of the crime or whether he knew what he was doing. He has an illness and he needs to be viewed that way.

"He needs to be contained within the legal system. No one is arguing that. Lock him up in the state mental hospital, where he can be studied and treated. Let him help the field of psychiatry. Study his brain and find out what happened to him. Do it non-intrusively through MRIs. He wasn't always killing people. Something happened to him. Let him get healthy enough and stable enough and he can tell you his story. We can use him to help others. He was very bright and he could contribute something to our understanding of these tragic events. He could work toward helping others prevent what happened to him.

"How many millions is Colorado spending on him and how many more millions will it spend on him throughout the course of his life? Put him to work. Give him a job. Give him a computer and access to books. He chose neuroscience as a career because he knew he was going offline. You don't just wake up one morning and become acutely psychotic. He went through a process and he's interested in how the brain works. He could be very useful in helping us comprehend how all this occurs inside of someone who becomes this violent. Holmes wanted to contribute to society by enrolling in the CU neuroscience program. He can still do that."

As the lawyers kept arguing in front of Judge Samour and the case kept getting further and further delayed, if not derailed, the *Aurora Sentinel* finally spoke up for the greater interest of the community. "Allowing the public," the newspaper's editors wrote, "to understand as much as possible about Holmes's state of mind only makes it easier to keep everyone on the road to a fair trial and justice. Right now, those in charge of this trial are lost."

Colorado v. James E. Holmes was on the verge of stalling out.

XXVIII

On January 14, 2014, young students in New Mexico were gathered inside Roswell's Berrendo Middle School gym waiting for their classes to start. A center for farming and ranching, Roswell has a population of around fifty thousand. In the gym that morning, the boys and girls heard a loud pop and saw blood flying and a fellow student lying on the floor—he'd just been shot in the face. One of their twelve year old classmates was holding a 22 gauge sawed off shotgun, waving it around, as panic spread through the gymnasium. An eleven-year-old boy was critically injured and a thirteen-year-old girl was also wounded but in stable condition.

John Masterson, an eighth-grade social studies teacher, immediately stepped in and confronted the shooter, the gun pointing directly at him. Masterson talked the boy into dropping his weapon, holding him until authorities arrived.

Before this incident, the Roswell Independent School District had prepared teachers and students for an "active shooter" situation, and some of the students had initially thought this attack was a surprise drill. The shooter, who'd sneaked the shotgun onto campus through a bag or musical instrument case, was arrested and transferred to an Albuquerque psychiatric hospital.

In the first fourteen school days of 2014, there were seven school shootings, compared to twenty-eight school shootings in all of 2013.

On January 21 at Purdue University, a twenty-three-year-old teaching assistant fired four shots inside a campus building, killing a twenty-one-year-old senior. The day before, a student was hospitalized after being shot near the athletic center on the campus of Widener University in Pennsylvania. The week before that, three other shootings led to the hospitalization of five students between the ages of twelve and eighteen. An eighth grader was arrested in Georgia after bringing a gun to school on consecutive days with the intention of robbing a classmate. In Portland, Oregon, police rushed to a local high school after a student displayed a gun to a fellow classmate during the lunch hour. And four teenagers were arrested for pointing a gun at a school bus in Norfolk, Virginia.

■ ■ ■

The numbers surrounding this phenomenon may be hard to absorb, but they're worth repeating. In the 1960s, there was one prominent school shooting. The 1980s saw twenty-seven of them. The 1990s had fifty-eight school shootings, and from 2000 until 2012 there were 102, an increase of more than 10,000 percent in just over fifty years. More than 70 percent of all the shooters since 2000 were born after 1980, and many of them were only fourteen or fifteen years old.

In the fourteen months since Newtown's Sandy Hook massacre, forty-four new shootings had erupted at schools, an average of more than three a month. The first six weeks of 2014 saw thirteen such shootings, and the majority took place inside K-12 schools.

"American schools have at times been a place for extreme shaming," says Mitchell Hall, the Holistic Health & Wellness coordinator and counselor at PsycheHealth, Ltd. in San Francisco. "It's an environment in which the few can be stars and the others are made to feel inferior or like failures. There's a lot of toxicity in these environments. The kids who erupt into violence hate themselves and are killing what they hate inside themselves. Some people ask: Why don't they just kill themselves? Their mass violence is their way of demonstrating their own torture and torment to the outside world—this is what the world did to me. People who don't heal from traumas often reenact them in the external world."

■ ■ ■

For nearly two decades, Kira Jones, a New Mexico native, has worked in education as a high school and community college teacher. She's taught all levels of special education, from gifted students to those with behavioral disorders. Currently, she's the Education Program Manager at the Santa Fe Art Institute. In 2011 and 2012, before settling in Santa Fe, she lived in Barcelona, Spain, with her five-year-old daughter. Her experience abroad was deeply informative. It wasn't the large contrasts between Spain and America that stayed with her, but the everyday ones, the smallest of interactions.

"When the James Holmes shooting happened," Kira says, "I'd just purchased a return ticket for us to come back to the States and to my aging parents. I didn't want us to be that far away from them. After the Aurora massacre, I was very conflicted about leaving Spain and sat up late at night thinking, *I'm not going back, I'm not going back.* Living in Barcelona was so much different from being in America. It's hard to describe all the differences and some might seem minor, but they all add up to what life is like in another culture.

"There isn't fast food in Barcelona, life isn't as hectic, and the elderly and the children and even the disabled are much more integrated into the life of the whole community. Everyone has his or her own support group. There are muggings on the subway, but not murders. There aren't mass shootings, which in America have become almost normal. It's very hard to get a gun in Barcelona. You have to go through an extensive and expensive mental health exam that you have to pay for. All your friends are interviewed to see if you're stable. When you talk to the local people about this, they don't bring up the difficulty of the process of getting a gun. They say, 'Why would anyone want to own one?'"

Just as it is very challenging to purchase a gun in Spain, in Germany certain violent videos are edited or not released at all, because the culture does not support this.

"Who would ever think or imagine that you were no longer safe sitting in a movie theater?" Jones says. "The people in Spain think that the people in America are insane because of the gun violence. It's a horrific mystery to them and they simply don't comprehend why we're doing this to ourselves. What struck me the most about living in Barcelona was that the people are not isolated as they are in the States. We all now have an image of a young male loner sitting in his basement on the computer buying weapons or planning something destructive. In Barcelona, you don't see people sitting alone in cafés or eating alone or walking alone or drinking alone at a bar. If you're alone and on your computer in a café, it's looked down on, especially if you're a foreigner. You feel shunned by the waiters. After a while, I began to feel ashamed in these situations because I wasn't interacting with others.

"In that culture, if you were ordering guns and ammo on a computer, or if you were acting very strangely, somebody would notice and they'd talk about it. Here people just slip through the cracks because no one is really paying attention. We're under so much financial pressure to keep up and under so many other pressures we've created that we don't take the time to interact in this way. These observations made a huge and lasting impression on me. It's a different kind of social interaction and community. You see young people walking with the elderly arm in arm.

"After Aurora, I thought there would be changes in the gun laws. After Newtown, I was certain there would be. Then I realized that our society doesn't yet have a tipping point—even these events didn't cause us to rethink what we're doing. It's still the Wild West. In New Mexico, you can walk into the state legislature with a gun. When I told people in Barcelona and ex-pats that I was going back to America to work on gun control, they said, 'It's too late. Why do you think we're living here instead of the States?'

"America was founded on individuality, on protecting your own territory, and on having your own rights and not being messed with. We still think and live that way. A lot of it comes down to economics. When people have health care and decent jobs and a sense of connectedness to their family and work, the stress and the isolation are much less. If we don't have these things and feel under increasing pressure to get them, or can't get them, some people will deteriorate and turn violent. It's just that basic. If we're all so busy looking out for ourselves, we don't notice the people who get lost and turn into a James Holmes or an Adam Lanza.

"After Sandy Hook, I could not stop thinking about those kids, who are the same age as my daughter. When I take her to school now, I realize this could be the last time I'll ever see her. She's in the first grade. Our political leaders are spineless on gun control. They're as disconnected from reality as the culture itself is. In Spain, if you run into somebody on the street and know them, you take the time to sit down for coffee or a drink. You talk and make a connection with something other than your iPhone. We've lost touch with our common humanity."

From a twenty-nine-year-old male in Texas:

> *Whenever I go over to my friends' homes and we're watching something on TV, I turn the sound off during the commercials. They think this is weird, but it's a sign of how much I dislike the consumer culture we live in. I feel that I'm in a constant struggle with American society over this issue. A long time ago, it became obvious to me that the things we're always told to value aren't really valued at all. Things like courage and honesty and being yourself when it's difficult to speak up and do that.*

XXIX

As the Holmes January 27 sanity hearing approached, two mental health experts met with Dr. Metzner to discuss his earlier examination of the defendant. The DA's office had already selected this duo to test Holmes again, if Judge Samour allowed that to happen. Psychologist Kris Mohandie worked with the FBI and psychiatrist Phillip Resnick had "been involved in just about every high-profile homicide case this country has seen" in recent decades, the judge would write of him. Some of these cases included that of Oklahoma City bomber Timothy McVeigh, serial killer Jeffrey Dahmer, and Unabomber Ted Kaczynski. The prosecution had already been paying Resnick $400 an hour and Mohandie $300 an hour for their opinions about the sanity of the defendant; so far, Mohandie had earned an estimated $45,000 for this work.

Mohandie and Resnick had both read and found problems with Metzner's report on Holmes. They felt that Metzner was biased, and they sought to study the defendant themselves. In the view of some legal professionals, the prosecution's desire to have their own hand-picked experts examine Holmes was justified, given that in Colorado, the state must prove that a defendant is sane.

Stan Garnett, the District Attorney for Boulder County, had been involved in numerous cases involving both sanity issues and the death penalty. In his county in 2010, Stephanie Rochester suffocated her six-month-old son because she feared he had autism. A state psychiatrist determined that the mother had a "major depressive disorder," and the judge declared Rochester not guilty by reason of insanity. Garnett disputed this and cited evidence that she'd tried to suffocate the baby over a period of hours, at one point going back to the dinner table to rejoin her husband after an unsuccessful attempt on the infant's life. The DA unsuccessfully appealed the judge's decision not to allow a prosecution expert to examine her.

"Because the defendant is the sole source of evidence in this situation," he said in his appeal, "courts have noted a defendant's opportunity to manipulate the information the prosecution receives."

In discussing the Holmes plea, Garnett said, "In many cases, because the defense is seeking the exam, the results will come back and say that the defendant is insane. The judge can then order a second evaluation from an independent examiner so you also have that opinion. But the prosecution can't have its own experts test the defendant. I think the state legislature should change this law to make things more fair, but defense attorneys would strongly oppose that.

"When the Holmes case occurred, I began hearing from prosecutors around the state who told me, 'We should have made these changes before this happened.' I'd change the law to say that both sides can examine the defendant. Then the jurors can hear all the evidence and make their own decision."

■ ■ ■

Dr. Metzner had devoted twenty-five hours to interviewing Holmes and roughly one hundred additional hours to speaking with witnesses and mental health personnel who'd talked with the defendant prior to the crime, and to digesting the scores of CDs and DVDs made about the young man. For weeks he'd focused his full professional attention on the case and reached his conclusions after much research and consideration. Before his only meeting with Mohandie and Resnick, he didn't understand that his comments to them might be used against him and to convince Judge Samour that Holmes needed further testing. After getting together with Mohandie and Resnick, he refused to see the prosecutors again because he felt "blindsided" and "set up" by them.

The sanity hearing lasted from January 27–30 and was at times testy. The mental health professionals were all fighting for their point of view about Holmes, while the judge refereed the conflict. As Mohandie and Resnick offered a detailed critique and criticism of Metzner, he became more upset and defensive, again feeling undermined by the prosecution team.

Three weeks later, Samour ruled that although he did not think Metzner had been biased when first testing Holmes, he'd now become biased because of his difficulties with the prosecution's psychiatrists. Given another chance to evaluate the prisoner, Metzner wouldn't be able to "resist the temptation" to prove that his initial findings had been accurate.

Prosecutors, he wrote, were requesting a second exam because "the prior experts' opinions were incomplete. That is, a potentially new and significant diagnosis had been proposed that could dramatically alter an assessment of the defendant's behavior on the day of the incident."

Samour ordered a second evaluation, to be conducted at the jail where Holmes was incarcerated or again at the hospital in Pueblo. He rejected the request by Mohandie and Resnick to do the follow-up exam, asking the Colorado Mental Health Institute to conduct a nationwide search for an independent psychiatric expert by March 10, 2014, a few weeks hence. The new report had to be completed by July 11, 2014, and the next evaluator had to answer only one question: Was Holmes insane at the time of the shootings?

The judge then set a new trial date of October 14, 2014, nearly twenty-seven months after the massacre. If that date held up, the first group

of *9,000 prospective jurors*—an unheard of number—would be sum-
moned to the Arapahoe County courthouse for voir dire, the question-
and-answer session leading to the selection of a jury. This process alone
could take several months and would involve the largest jury pool
ever called before the start of an American trial. This number might
have seemed like overkill, but given the parameters of the case, and
the extreme circumstances each juror would have to confront, it also
seemed justified. Some portion of those nine thousand potential jurors
called likely knew one of the victims, or their families, or one of 223
officers who'd come to the crime scene or one of the first responders
at the theater, or one of the medical personnel at the hospitals where
the wounded were taken. Also, the jury had to be "death qualified,"
meaning that they would not only pass judgment on Holmes's guilt
or innocence but also commit themselves to deciding whether he lived
or was executed. Finally, they had to be available to sit through four
or five months of legal proceedings for fifty dollars a day. They would
be presented with gruesome forensic and photographic evidence of the
carnage inside the theater. Even after casting such a wide net over the
jury pool, the various hardships the potential jurors were facing were
certain to cause many of them to be dismissed.

As soon as the judge ordered a second evaluation, the defense said
that they'd challenge this decision in the Colorado Supreme Court.
They did, and they lost. Legal commentators said the trial wouldn't
start now until early 2015, which turned out to be accurate, but not
before the defense would try to postpone it several more times.

■ ■ ■

A year earlier, virtually all of the relevant facts of the case had become
known, but something was missing. The facts did not add up to the
truth—not the whole truth. That lay elsewhere, hidden in the pages of
the spiral notebook or the defendant's words to Dr. Metzner or in the
testimony of Dr. Metzner himself. More than a year and a half after

the massacre, the gag order remained in place and the case felt frozen. In any murder trial, this would have been troubling. But in this case, it felt like something more than that.

From the beginning, the Aurora shootings had stood out as an educational opportunity for those trying to understand more about America's mass-shooting phenomenon. All of the elements were in place. The defendant had chosen to live instead of die in police gunfire or commit suicide at the theater. He was highly intelligent and had been a PhD candidate in neuroscience. Holmes had likely been studying his own mind and/or mental illness in grad school. He'd written extensively in his spiral notebook about his inner life in the months leading up to the murders. He'd spoken with a psychiatrist at the University of Colorado who specialized in what may have been plaguing him—the onset of schizophrenia—which tended to affect some men in their twenties. He'd given information to another mental health expert, Dr. Metzner, yet no one could speak about any of this in a public way, a way that might illuminate the phenomenon of mass violence committed by American youth.

Nearly two years after the shootings, the legal system had made it impossible to extract any pertinent psychological data from the tragedy. The division and conflict pervading the culture that had produced Holmes had infected everything and everyone in the courtroom.

The defense now asked for a change of venue for the trial and attacked the Twitter feeds of Rob McCallum, the public information officer for Colorado's Eighteenth Judicial District. They disliked McCallum's "jovial tweets" with a prosecutor, his exchanges with journalists, and his announcements about press conferences or responses to inquiries from non-news sources.

The eighteen-page criticism of McCallum prompted Jeremy Meyer of *The Denver Post* to write, "The Holmes case is one of the most intriguing in the country and is being watched internationally. McCallum has handled the crush of media interest with aplomb and has not endangered the case with his Twitter feed. Last year, McCallum was even awarded the Sue O'Brien Award for Public Service by the Colorado Freedom of Information Coalition . . ."

The case, Meyer argued, hadn't been undermined by Rob McCallum, but by an "overreaching gag order," which had kept the Aurora Police Department from publicly discussing their tactics on the night of the crime when loading their patrol cars with wounded victims because ambulances couldn't get close enough to the theater. Other cities had sought to learn from Aurora's law enforcement experience, but the APD couldn't provide them with this information until a court order allowed this in the fall of 2014. Likewise, the surviving victims who were suing the Century 16 Theater owners had also been denied access to critical transcripts and exhibits that had already been exposed during Holmes's preliminary hearing.

Meyer was pleased when the judge chose not to punish McCallum. Yet Samour did use this incident to remind everyone that the strict gag order remained in place. "He didn't need to say that," Meyer concluded. "We already were gagging."

■ ■ ■

In late May, as Judge Samour was denying the defense's change-of-venue motion, twenty-two-year-old Elliot Rodger, the son of a Hollywood director, went on a stabbing and shooting spree across the seaside California college community of Isla Vista. Enraged after being rejected by young women he'd wanted to date, Rodger killed two females and four males, all of them students at the University of California, Santa Barbara. Another thirteen people were injured before Rodger shot and killed himself inside his BMW. He posted on YouTube a "Day of Retribution" video right before the assault. He also wrote a 140-page manifesto, outlining his wounded feelings and desire to extract revenge.

Right after the massacre, Richard Martinez, whose twenty-year-old son Christopher had died in the rampage, held a press conference. He was so distraught that he could barely force out his words: "Why did

Chris die? Chris died because of craven, irresponsible politicians and the NRA. They talk about gun rights. What about Chris's right to live? When will this insanity stop? When will enough people say, 'Stop this madness; we don't have to live like this?' Too many have died. We should say to ourselves: not one more."

Responding to Martinez, Samuel Joseph Wurzelbacher (who'd become nationally known as "Joe the Plumber" during the 2008 presidential campaign) wrote an open letter to the grieving parents of the people Rodger had killed: "I am sorry you lost your child. I myself have a son and daughter and the one thing I never want to go through is what you are going through now. But as harsh as this sounds—your dead kids don't trump my Constitutional rights."

Martinez's comments about the NRA and politicians, he said, "will be exploited by gun-grab extremists as are all tragedies involving gun violence and the mentally ill by the anti-Second Amendment Left . . . It is my responsibility to protect my family" and "[I] will stand up for that right vehemently."

Because Elliott Rodger had targeted young women (and men), the shootings inspired a social media movement that immediately sprang up around women's issues. Called #YesAllWomen, it went viral and amassed 1.5 million tweets in its first three days.

Once again, America's undeclared civil war had been highlighted by the violence of a twentysomething male from a privileged background.

A few weeks later, Aaron Ybarra, a twenty-six-year-old armed with an AK-47 and other weapons, including a knife, opened fire at Seattle Pacific University, killing one person and wounding three more.

■ ■ ■

According to the periodical *Awareness*, the single biggest common factor in nearly all recent mass shootings was that the killers were either taking psychotropic drugs or had been doing so in the not-too-distant past. The periodical mentioned scientific studies and pharmaceutical companies' internal documents showing that SSRI drugs (Selective Serotonin Re-Uptake Inhibitors) have clearly known, but basically unreported, side effects, including suicide and other violent behavior. Counting Elliot Rodger's massacre at Isla Vista, thirty-three school shootings and/or school-related acts of violence had been committed by those taking or getting off of psychiatric drugs—acts that had left 177 people wounded and eighty-three dead. The mass shooters linked to psychotropic drugs—to quote from just a partial list of names provided by *Awareness*—included:

▶ Seventeen-year-old Eric Harris (on Zoloft and then Luvox) and eighteen-year-old Dylan Klebold, who killed twelve students, one teacher, and themselves at Columbine High School.

▶ Sixteen-year-old Jeff Weise was on 60 mg/day of Prozac—three times the normal starting dose for adults—when he murdered his grandfather, his grandfather's girlfriend, and his fellow students at Red Lake, Minnesota, before killing himself. He left a total of ten dead and twelve wounded.

▶ Sixteen-year-old Cory Baadsgaard of Wahluke (Washington State) High School was on Paxil when he held twenty-three classmates hostage with a rifle. He retained no memory of doing this.

▶ Thirteen-year-old Chris Fetters killed his favorite aunt while taking Prozac.

▶ Twelve-year-old Christopher Pittman murdered both his grandparents while taking Zoloft.

▶ Thirteen-year-old Mathew Miller hanged himself in his bedroom closet after taking Zoloft for six days.

▶ Fifteen-year-old Kip Kinkel, on both Prozac and Ritalin, shot his parents and then opened fire at his school, killing two classmates and injuring twenty-two shortly after starting on Prozac.

- Sixteen-year-old Luke Woodham was on Prozac when he killed his mother and two students, wounding six others.

- Fourteen-year-old Michael Carneal was on Ritalin when he fired on students at a high school prayer meeting in West Paducah, Kentucky. Three teenagers were killed and five others were wounded.

- Eleven-year-old Andrew Golden and fourteen-year-old Mitchell Johnson were on Ritalin when they shot fifteen people—killing four students and a teacher and wounding ten others.

- Fifteen-year-old T. J. Solomon was on Ritalin when he opened fire and wounded six classmates.

- Fourteen-year-old Rod Mathews was on Ritalin when he beat a classmate to death with a bat.

- Nineteen-year-old James Wilson was on multiple psychiatric drugs when he went into an elementary school with a .22-caliber revolver and killed two young girls, while wounding seven other children and two teachers.

- Thirteen-year-old Elizabeth Bush was on Paxil when she unleashed a school shooting in Pennsylvania.

- Jason Hoffman was on Effexor and Celexa during a school shooting in El Cajon, California.

- Seventeen-year-old Julie Woodward was on Zoloft when she hanged herself in her family's garage.

In early June 2014, as the second anniversary of the Aurora shootings approached, the *Albuquerque News* published an article that began, "Young killers have brains that differ considerably from those of male adolescents who have committed other types of serious crimes." The Mind Research Network at the University of New Mexico had looked at MRI brain scans of young male offenders and determined with an 81 percent degree of accuracy the brains of those who'd killed, according to Kent Kiehl, the lead author of the first in-depth neuro-scientific examination of the brain differences in teens who murder. Kiehl found that the killers had reduced gray matter in regions deep in the brain, where emotions are processed and impulses are regulated. The regions appeared to show delayed development in teens who commit homicide.

A few days after the study was released, thirty-one-year-old Jerad Miller gunned down two Las Vegas police officers at CiCi's pizza north of the Strip and an armed civilian in a nearby Walmart. Videos made prior to the massacre depicted his face painted to look like The Joker's. He was aided in the killings by his twenty-two-year-old wife, Amanda, and both had embraced extreme beliefs against what they saw as the tyrannical American government. The police shot and killed Jerad, while Amanda committed suicide.

Referring to the roughly thirty thousand gun deaths a year in America, including homicides and suicides, *Truthout* wrote, "The shooting of women by misogynist men, and the shooting of children in schools, and even the shooting of police officers having lunch, is doing far more to destroy the United States than a terrorist group ever could . . . We have met the terrorists threatening our national security. They are here in the homeland, empowered with legal standing to terrorize. This nation spends hundreds and hundreds of billions of dollars annually to 'fight terrorism abroad' . . . while U.S. domestic agencies let the terrorism within fester without constraint."

As these words were published, the American population watched Iraq being torn into fragments by fighting on several different fronts. The militant group ISIS would soon start beheading journalists and others and releasing videos of these events to the world. From

2003–2011, 4,486 U.S. soldiers had died fighting in Iraq, sent off to war on the Bush administration's repeated belief that Saddam Hussein had weapons of mass destruction. None were ever found, and once the United States began leaving that country after 2011, Iraq started its long descent into chaos. Bullying and violence had not worked abroad, and there was absolutely no evidence that it was working at home.

■ ■ ■

In midsummer 2014, Dr. William Reid, the second psychiatrist to examine James Holmes, told the court that the results of his testing would not be ready by the court-mandated deadline of July 11. Dr. Reid needed several more months, so the October 2014 date for the start of the trial had to be pushed back once again. The new trial date was December 8, 2014, but that wouldn't hold up either.

While these delays unfolded, the lawyers now tried to keep the public from being able to watch the Holmes trial, should it ever commence. *The Aurora Sentinel* was having none of it. "Arguments against a televised Holmes trial," the newspaper's editors wrote, "pale in comparison to the American public's compelling and overwhelming need to see this vital case unfold for itself. The entire country is the jury that will decide where we go from here. Anything less is less than justice served."

As the second anniversary of the Aurora shootings came that July, actor Christian Bale wrote a letter supporting more gun control: "My heart sank when I heard the news about the shooting two years ago in a movie theater in Aurora, Colorado. It was opening day of *The Dark Knight Rises* and twelve people had just been shot and killed at a midnight showing—fifty-eight wounded. The only thing I could think to do was go to Aurora. I visited the survivors and family members in the hospital.

"One of the amazing survivors of the shooting I met was Steve Barton—a guy who just happened to be passing through on a cross-country bike trip when he stopped to go to the movies with friends.

Tomorrow marks two years since the Aurora shooting. After the shooting, Steve focused his incredible talents on fighting for public safety measures that will prevent others' lives from being affected by gun violence like his was. I'm inspired by his resilience and dedication.

"The fact is, there's a lot more we can do to cut down on gun violence. After the Aurora shooting, Colorado passed a strong law that has already blocked criminals from easily buying guns without a background check. But making that kind of progress in other states or at the federal level is going to require elected officials with the backbone to act. That's why it's so important to support local, state, and federal candidates who will push for common-sense gun laws.

"On this sad anniversary, let's all recommit ourselves to turning tragedy into meaning. Watch Steve's powerful message now and then spread the word:

http://every.tw/aurora-two-years

"It's an honor to stand with Steve, with you and with all Americans fighting to reduce gun violence.

"Thank you, Christian Bale."

■ ■ ■

Others like Bale, operating outside the political and legal arenas, were trying to make a difference. Bill and Melinda Gates donated a million dollars to the Washington Alliance for Gun Responsibility, which was committed to lowering violence in the Evergreen State. The group backed Initiative 594, requiring criminal background checks on all firearms sales and transfers in Washington, including those on the Internet and at gun shows. "We believe," the couple said in a statement after offering their financial support for Initiative 594, "it will be an effective and balanced approach to improving gun safety in our state by closing existing loopholes for background checks."

In 2012, the gun-control movement was $285 million behind the gun-rights movement in terms of fund raising, but Aurora and Newtown began to change the momentum in this battle. The citizen activities following the Holmes and the Lanza massacres included a national, multimedia, investigative reporting project, run by News21, called "Gun Wars: The Struggle Over Rights and Regulation in America."

In 2005, the Carnegie Corporation of New York and the John S. and James L. Knight Foundation came together to start News21 as part of the Carnegie-Knight Initiative on the Future of Journalism Education. News21 was headquartered at the Walter Cronkite School of Journalism and Mass Communication at Arizona State University and engaged leading college journalism students from coast to coast in its projects. After studying the financing of the gun control movement, News21 reported in 2014 that it was beginning to catch up with the gun-rights crowd. Organizations like Everytown for Gun Safety and the Michael Bloomberg-backed Mayors Against Illegal Guns (MAIG) campaign were at least attempting to even up the score on the economic front.

At an Everytown event in Washington, DC, in May 2014, Shannon Watts, the founder of the gun control group Moms Demand Action for Gun Sense in America, said, "Now, for the first time in our country's history, there is a well-financed and formidable force positioned to take on the Washington gun lobby."

In mid-September 2014, The Brady Center to Prevent Gun Violence and Sandy and Lonnie Phillips, whose daughter, Jessica Ghawi, was killed at the Aurora theater, sued the online retailer who sold James Holmes body armor and ammunition used in the shootings. It was the first lawsuit ever against cyber sellers of ammunition and military equipment. Holmes bought ammunition and body armor from various online retailers, including bulkammo.com. The plaintiffs alleged that the websites "negligently supplied Holmes with the arsenal" and failed "to use any screening mechanism to determine his identity or intent for the products."

America's legal system may have been paralyzed, but its citizens were not. The first step toward taking action was seeing oneself not merely as a victim of these tragic circumstances, but as someone with the power to create change. Small steps might lead to larger ones later on.

In mid-November, those in Nevada promoting gun-owner background checks turned in slightly under 247,000 signatures for a 2016 state ballot measure to strengthen screening and reporting of weapon purchases. Nevadans for Background Checks want their state to become the eighteenth to require universal background checks for all sales and transfers of firearms.

Interlude

The preliminary hearing for James Holmes had been held back in early January 2013. The prosecution had its first opportunity to present some of its evidence, and then Judge Sylvester would decide if there was enough for Holmes to go on trial (in this particular case, the hearing was merely a formality that both sides had to go through; nobody doubted that Sylvester would bind the young man over for trial).

We asked Eric to join us at the hearing and watch the legal system in action, something he'd never done before. Many parents have one day a year when they can take their kids to the office and show them how they make a living. Since we were self-employed and worked at home, we'd never been able to do this; going to court with him would be something akin to that. He agreed to come along, and we all bundled up for the trip out to the Arapahoe County Justice Center. A large group of media and spectators wanted to attend the proceeding, and all of us had to stand outside at dawn in the bitter cold and ice to see if we'd get a seat in the courtroom. Fortunately, the three of us did, and we crowded in next to several people around Eric's age, a few of whom were there to support the defendant. Brightly colored spiked hair, black clothing, tattoos, and attitude were on full display.

Eric watched the morning session before telling us that he was driving back to the house in his own car. The details of the case, the forensic evidence, and the other things his parents had been sitting in courthouses and absorbing for the past couple of decades didn't interest him much. A little police testimony about what Holmes had actually done inside the theater was enough for him. He was more interested in the society and culture that had produced Holmes than in the physical results of the rampage. As he'd told us more than once, his generation had grown up with this kind of violence and was more or less inured to it. They'd never been aware of an America that wasn't at war somewhere in the world or wasn't home to these mass shootings and had come to accept all of this as nearly normal.

■ ■ ■

Something else Eric repeatedly told us was that his male friends didn't pay a lot of attention to books. They played video games, watched movies and documentaries, and viewed brief film clips online; outside of the classroom, they didn't read many books for recreation or plea-sure. They were too busy or their focus was elsewhere. The instant gratification of new forms of media had greater appeal than spending hours reading about one thing intently.

This wasn't what we wanted to hear, but if you practice investiga-tive journalism long enough, you get used to confronting obstacles in front of you.

"If your work was easy," someone had told us a long time ago, "everybody would be doing it."

Our son was good at raising sticky questions, and one of them flowed from this observation: If we were trying to write something about people his age, but they didn't read books, how did we expect to accomplish anything? It was all part of the larger challenge of taking on this very difficult subject matter. Many older people also didn't want to know the details of what Holmes had done or want to think about the mass-shooting phenomenon.

Sometimes, we were asked to speak publicly about the books we'd written. When we brought up the James Holmes case at these gatherings, one person or more inevitably said something like, "Why is it taking so long for him to go to trial? Why do we have to go through all this? Why don't they just kill him? Why don't they line him up in front of the police and shoot him or electrocute him or hang him or give him a lethal injection or do whatever they do to people like him now? Why all the waiting? Everyone knows he's guilty, so why can't we just get rid of him?"

The longer the Holmes defense team avoided going to trial, the more people naturally became frustrated with the delays, and the more of these comments we heard. Coloradans didn't understand a legal system that devoted years to bringing a confessed killer to trial. They didn't grasp why lawyers would fight for so long over a definition of legal sanity or insanity. They didn't see any reason to take months to select a jury for an obviously guilty man. They didn't like paying for all this, especially when they hadn't yet seen any results. But there was more to their grumblings than that. Fundamentally, they didn't understand mass shootings, were appalled by them, and wanted them to go away and never come back. They were reluctant to talk about this, and at the start of our conversations about Holmes, we usually heard things like:

"If we just didn't have to think about these tragedies anymore . . . If these kids would straighten up or if they'd go off somewhere and shoot themselves and leave the rest of us alone . . . They've had all the advantages in life, and now they're doing *this* to the rest of us?"

All of this reflected the profound American desire for a quick, easy, and sanitary resolution to things . . . Just line him up against a wall and shoot him.

Yet if we didn't stop there, if we kept the discussion alive, we could eventually break through this initial resistance and engage with people on the issue. They'd start to listen and to ask questions and to share their own ideas and feelings, which were always more complicated than take him out and kill him in order to cut the taxpayers' expense, which could easily run into the millions. Gradually, they'd begin to see themselves as part of this new and disturbing reality, instead of being totally removed from it or just victimized by it.

From a different direction, in the off-Broadway Barrow Street Theater in New York City, British comedian Jonny Donahoe was putting on a one-man show about mental illness called *Every Brilliant Thing*. Before each performance he walked through the audience and gave everyone a slip of paper containing a phrase like "ice cream" or "water fights"—little reminders that his on-stage character used to help cheer up his suicidal mother. In trying to engage people in a very uncomfortable subject, Donahoe asked them to become part of the show and to act out various roles with him. He employed humor to get them to connect with a painful reality.

"I think that's just the best way you can deal with it," he said in an interview with National Public Radio, "not just in a show, but as a human being . . . You are going to, whoever you are, at some point experience mental health issues, whether that is because you suffer from them yourself or your partner does or your parents. But it's too common for it to pass you by."

In our own way, we were trying to do something similar. We weren't telling others that we had the answers to the confounding tragedies caused by mass shootings; we were simply trying to start a conversation, and to identify some of the problems, and to pose the right questions. Maybe they could help us do that. Maybe our dialogue could be useful. Maybe they could be part of our journey in writing this book.

What emerged from this was the realization that no one had ever talked with these people in any depth about this subject. While communities across America were being shattered by these shootings, those we spoke to felt no sense of community around this phenomenon. No one had asked them to participate in any kind of give-and-take about it, until now. No one had wanted to know what they thought or felt. Everyone had wanted to ignore the issue.

The underlying truth was that the challenges in America today weren't like those in the past, when there was often a clear and obvious enemy. Now we were fighting ourselves in ways that didn't make any sense, at least on the surface. If people could see themselves as having some involvement in these events, they began to open up about this wrenching topic and to think more about being a citizen in a troubled but participatory democracy. They began to use their intelligence and empathy instead of offering the kneejerk reaction of using violence to get rid of the rampant violence we were seeing everywhere.

And they began to realize something more pervasive and subtle: There was no leadership for dealing with any of this. No politician wanted to touch the subject and no religious leader, either, for that matter. The silence around the shootings had accomplished nothing. We were confronting something new, and that meant having to think about it in a new way. And that meant that everyone needed to contribute to the solution.

■ ■ ■

Without the start of a critical discussion in America about why young men commit mass shootings and the culture of violence that subtly justifies this behavior, there was no indication it would stop. Change starts when people realize they have choices—when they can say or do or explore what they hadn't thought about exploring before. Change begins when they can see alternatives that they'd never thought about before.

No issue in America was more in need of alternative thinking, and alternative actions and strategies, than the mass-shooting phenomenon. There were people who'd quietly been working in that direction for years.

MINDFULNESS

XXX

When Bidyut Bose was a child in Calcutta, his father taught him yoga and took him to the Himalayas to meet yogis and discuss the purpose of life. Although the elder Bose was a materials scientist who'd worked in America, he wanted his son to be rooted in the spiritual traditions of the East. He introduced the boy to monks who embodied the idea of "selfless service," devoting themselves to disaster relief or to helping orphanages and health clinics across India. The monks' teachings and their concept of this service became an ingrained part of the young man's consciousness. In 1977, after getting his undergraduate education in computer science, Bidyut (who prefers to be called BK) came to the United States for graduate school at Pittsburgh's Carnegie Mellon University. He earned a master's degree in the same field and took a job in Northern California's Silicon Valley, while getting a PhD at Berkeley.

BK then returned to India to work in social services in the country's poor rural areas. He formed a small non-profit that supported sustainable agriculture and low-cost housing, but while the work was satisfying and fulfilled what he'd absorbed from his father and the monks, he was torn between staying in his homeland and returning to the States to pursue his career in the field of high-tech. He eventually went back to California and got a job in computer research and development, but was still not quite satisfied. He was making money and advancing at work but felt that what he did for a living and his deeper purpose in life were not yet aligned. He was too removed from the concept of "selfless service."

During all of his travels and educational opportunities and jobs, he observed the same thing everywhere: Human beings were under significant stress, sometimes chronic stress, and the effects of this on them were important—not to mention his own chronic stress. "I saw a lot of people in America going after millions of dollars," he says. "They were so driven at work that they slept on their office floors or couches in order to earn more money and stock options. They were bright and successful, but something was missing. They all had something in common: high levels of stress. I decided to become a serious student of stress and started to look at the neuroscience of stress and at what might be an optimal treatment response for chronic stress."

The problems were in all socio-economic groups. In the Bay Area's upscale Palo Alto neighborhoods, teens were cutting themselves because they felt under so much pressure. In the rougher parts of Oakland, young people were often trapped in the drop-out-of-school-to-prison pipeline. "The school-to-prison pipeline," Bose has written about his research into chronic stress, "is populated with a disproportionately high number of youth of color. And in communities with disproportionate minority populations, there is disproportionately higher stress and trauma . . . Epigenetics tells us that stress affects us down to our DNA and that our gene maps have chemical markers called tags, which respond to chronic stress . . . Public health data show that stress is the single common effect of every major social determinant of health, such as income inequality, institutionalized racism, and the breakdown of traditional family structures . . ."

He outlined the four areas where stress most significantly affected the brain: attention control, emotion regulation, healthy coping, and empathy. Both creative thinking and learning were impaired by a lack of attention. Regulating emotions, or failing to, affected everything people do—from the entertainment they choose to explore to what they eat to those they spend time with to what they think and talk about. The more BK studied the problem, the more he saw not just the emotional cost of all this, but the financial price as well: the billions in expense from kids dropping out of school and ending up in prison. One in two students from inner-city neighborhoods quit school without graduating, and a lot of them ended up in jail. The more he studied stress, the more he understood that the great majority of these young people had not come of age in isolation from their social circumstances, but were products of the social forces surrounding them. His mission in life, he decided, and his commitment to selfless service would revolve around understanding the school to prison pipeline.

Neuroscience showed him that compared to the rest of the body, the brain was the most responsive to its environment; it was far more malleable and plastic than, for example, the heart or the skin or other organs. The environment one lived in—with all of its social, racial, and economic components—and the brain's response to that environment had a major impact on health. The formula was quite simple: the greater the stress of that environment, the worse the outcomes.

"Many kids who are chronically stressed out," he says, "are not ready to learn in school. You can't teach them until you first deal with this condition. I'm just blown away by how much anger they hold in their little bodies. We're rushing to teach them to learn before we help them to heal, and that isn't working."

Not only did neuroscience reveal the problems underlying stress, it also gave BK some possible solutions. Neuroscience indicated that what he calls "mindfulness practices" could mitigate each of these negatives. Change the brain's response to its environment, even without being able to change that environment itself, and you could change behaviors. You did this through repetitive practices, the same way you learned any other skill or trained any other muscle.

"Through mindfulness," he says, "you can change the neuronal patterns and synaptic firings of the brain. You can do this through mental training of the brain, just as you can do it for other body parts.

You can do it through mindfulness, which is a fairly new term in our lexicon. Mindfulness means to fill the mind with the present, not the past or the future. You can do it by sitting meditation to deal with stress and trauma, but you're more affected by meditation in which you move the body. When you sit, stress bubbles up within you and you hold onto it. When you use your body, you can relieve these feelings. This is what I call 'mindfulness in motion.' And that is what yoga is. It integrates mindfulness, movement, and breathing."

He defines mindfulness as "being aware of what we are doing as we are doing it, aware of what we are feeling as we are feeling it, and aware of what we are thinking just as we are thinking it . . . The latest trauma research shows that our bodies hold trauma in our tissues and that physical movement is essential for dissolving trauma."

■ ■ ■

After leaving Silicon Valley at the end of the 1990s, BK devoted the next half decade to looking in depth at the neuroscience of stress and reading studies about it. He successfully employed his concepts at a cancer hospital, but wanted to extend them into the school system, especially to teenagers dropping out of high school and ending up inside the criminal justice system. To reach the minority community, he first had to "change the address of yoga. I wanted to move it from the affluence of Palo Alto to the iron corridors of inner-city Oakland." Many of the latter kids came from abuse or neglect at home and had grown up immersed in crime, drugs, gangs, guns, and frequent killings in their communities. The data revealed what was undeniable: The stress driving students to misbehavior or violence came from the environmental conditions they were surrounded by. In one of the studies BK encountered, 98 percent of the students in a particular school qualified for a diagnosis of post-traumatic stress disorder (PTSD).

But there was resistance. Black and Latino kids associated yoga with upper-middle-class white women—not a good starting place for drawing them in—so BK had to find another opening. He'd discovered that many major sports stars were also practicing yoga, and this piece of news carried some weight and street cred in the neighborhoods he wanted to impact. If a pro basketball or football legend was doing yoga, it couldn't be all bad.

When you regulate emotion, BK's research had shown, you then have the capacity to align the body, the brain stem, the limbic system, and the prefrontal cortex. The reptilian brain comes from the stem; the limbic system holds memory, desire, fear, and past trauma. The prefrontal cortex deals with concepts and the more complicated thought processes. If he could bring all these into alignment in students, he believed that attention would improve and learning would come more naturally.

In 2005, he and a business partner, Judy Dunlap, decided to launch an urban training center called "Niroga" in the Bay Area. In Sanskrit, "roga" means disease and "ni" means the absence of something. Together the two words mean "well-being in the broadest possible sense." Niroga's purpose was to use what BK had learned during five years of researching chronic stress to try to help the at-risk population of young people in Oakland. To assist him, he engaged (pro bono) the services of the WSGR law firm, which helped the two partners form their business.

"In starting Niroga," he says, "I'd clarified my intention about what I wanted to accomplish and to give back through selfless service, and then everything supported this project and came together for us. I began to see in my own life what I'd seen in the teachers and teachings of those yogis my father had exposed me to in my youth. I came into alignment with my own deeper purpose."

In Orlando, Florida, he made a presentation to four hundred education leaders about helping their target population of at-risk kids who had disproportionally higher stress. He explained how "mindful action" and "mindful breathing" could transform them from the inside out. He then took his program to Alameda County Juvenile Hall. After learning that the average stay at the Hall was three weeks, he told those running the organization that he had two conditions he wouldn't compromise on. He insisted on working with the kids five days a week—not one or two or three as the facility was suggesting. He also insisted that he had to teach the staff as well as the incarcerated youth. He wasn't trying just to change the kids, but to alter the culture of the institution, and that meant reaching everyone who worked there. Finally, he wanted to be able to measure the impact he was having.

"The staff hemmed and hawed about all of this," he says, "but they eventually agreed to these terms. When we started, the kids were very skeptical: we don't do yoga, that sort of thing. It was a big hurdle, but we overcame it. We told the young men that athletes were doing this and told the young women that it would improve their body image. We told all of them that it would help them manage their stress."

A major California foundation approached BK about his program with juveniles and offered to help him evaluate the impact of the program. Could he really lower stress and increase self-control through yoga? His research with the kids revealed a statistically significant decrease in stress and heightened emotional regulation and self-control. He found that self-control was a better predictor of outcomes for substance abuse and emotional regulation. It was also a more accurate predictor of academic achievement than IQ. He put together a 440-page book with forty-eight yoga lessons, which could be implemented over a sixteen-week school semester.

While this program had worked in juvenile hall, what would happen once the kids were released? He offered free yoga sessions in the community, but the youth he'd connected with in juvenile hall didn't show up. He decided that the best place to reach the fourteen- to eighteen-year-olds was in school, and he implemented his plan at El Cerrito High. It had funding for fifteen classrooms, and BK installed the program for three times or more a week, at fifteen minutes per session. The students did a series of yoga poses and breathing on a consistent basis.

"Even these small interventions done regularly enough," he says, "will produce change that we could measure. As we continued to bring this work into the classroom, we began getting requests for training from around the country and beyond. We worked with the U.N. in Palestine's West Bank to help those people—three classes a week for stress management, self-awareness, and emotional regulation."

BK then expanded his work to a San Diego elementary school and began exploring other opportunities across the nation. "We teach them more than yoga," he says. "We teach people to act rather than merely *re*act and to start building healthy relationships. This is really all about exploring the foundational parts of yoga. Yoga means to 'yoke' yourself and to connect with who you really are.

"We're quite good at exploring and implementing changes in our external environment, such as creating more gun control, but we're not so good at changing our internal environments. The solutions to our problems with violence will be optimal when we have a better balance between the two. We want to internalize these self-awareness and self-management skills in young people. This is not a random process, but a systemic change to how we teach people a better way to live. When Gandhi said, 'Be the change you want to see in the world,' the most important word was not *change*, but *be*. We have to start looking at new ways of interacting with ourselves first and then others."

When one of the local police chiefs became aware of the success of BK's program, his response was unqualified: "This kind of change is a matter of life and death on my streets."

XXXI

Each week, the Niroga Institute taught yoga to more than two thousand children in schools, juvenile halls, alternative schools, and jails throughout the Bay Area. Niroga's main focus was on minority youth at high risk for school failure and delinquency, but it also conducted Transformative Life/Leadership Skills (TLS) trainings for parents, mental health professionals, community partners, social workers, educators, and criminal justice and violence prevention officials. The training sessions offered yoga postures, breathing techniques, and meditation to help adults care for at-risk youth. In Alameda County, the education, health care, and probation departments all supported Niroga's Juvenile Hall yoga program, while Bay Area school districts began funding it as well. It was a fully coordinated community project, and students in the program demonstrated lower levels of stress and greater levels of self-control, more involvement at school, and more emotional awareness.

After a family court judge brought Niroga in to conduct a TLS training at a Delaware school district, the judge wanted to know more. He told BK that this program could "help dismantle" the school-to-prison pipeline; he hoped to see it installed in schools nationwide.

BK promoted yoga not just as a healing technique, but as an "economic imperative." Nearly one million American youth quit school each year and another million were detained in juvenile halls. In the inner city, dropout rates exceed 50 percent and recidivism for juveniles is nearly 75 percent. The lifetime cost of a single high-school dropout is estimated at $250,000, so the overall annual price tag for school failure in the United States is roughly $260 billion. Yoga costs about a $1,000 annually per student, and with $250,000, Niroga could provide yoga to 250 youth for a year. If just one of them stayed in school and out of juvenile hall, the program would break even. If 10 percent did this, the return on investment would be twenty-six-fold.

BK and Niroga want to supplement the three Rs of reading, writing, and arithmetic with a fourth R—"reflective capacity for enhancing resilience and self-reliance, self-awareness, and self-mastery"—which he views as essential for preparing children for the twenty-first century. He's calling for systematic yoga training for school-based behavioral health professionals and for teachers in inner-city public schools across the country.

"If even a fraction of the resources that we spend on incarceration," he's written, "could be spent on transforming our internal environments (stress management and healing from trauma), the social return would be substantial."

■ ■ ■

Mainstream science has begun to support what BK had been promoting in the Bay Area and beyond. In the spring of 2014, John Denninger, a Harvard Medical School psychiatrist, led a government-funded, five-year study on how yoga and meditation affect genes and brain activity in the chronically stressed. The National Institutes of Health was providing $3.3 million for Denninger to track 210 healthy subjects with high levels of stress for six months. Decades earlier, Denninger became involved in these ancient practices while visiting China and working with a tai chi master. He pursued this interest first as an undergrad at Harvard and later as the director of research at the Benson-Henry Institute for Mind Body Medicine at Massachusetts General Hospital, one of Harvard's teaching hospitals.

In 2013, he published a work documenting how "mind-body techniques" switch on and off certain genes linked to stress and immune function. Earlier studies had shown the benefits of these techniques, but mostly by using participant questionnaires or heart rate and blood pressure monitoring. Denninger was employing more refined technology provided by neuro-imaging and genomics, which could measure the physiological changes in greater detail. The new results established, as he puts it, "a true biological effect."

The significance of this effect was hard to exaggerate. According to the Benson-Henry Institute, stress affects everything from infertility to aging—and accounts for 60–90 percent of doctor's visits in the United States. The World Health Organization estimates that stress costs American companies at least $300 billion a year through low-productivity, absenteeism, and turnover.

The studies of chronic stress, as BK had hoped while working at Niroga, are emerging alongside a so-called "mindfulness movement," which includes meditation and yoga and claims such devotees as comedian Jerry Seinfeld and media mogul Rupert Murdoch. In another 2013 study, UCLA scientists and Nobel Prize–winner Elizabeth Blackburn documented that just twelve minutes of daily yoga/ meditation for eight weeks increased telomerase activity by 43 percent. Telomerase is known as the "immortality enzyme," because it slows the cellular aging process.

A Tulane University School of Medicine study, published online in a 2014 spring issue of the journal *Pediatrics*, found that the more children were affected by domestic violence or trauma—like the suicide or incarceration of a family member—the more likely their DNA would be altered by the experience. These kids demonstrated shorter telomeres, a cellular marker of aging, compared to children in more stable households. Shorter telomeres are linked to higher risks for mental illness, diabetes, obesity, and heart disease.

One's physical and emotional environments had a direct impact on one's genetic structure. The trauma went just that deep. Undoing the trauma took more than wanting it to go away.

In November 2014, Prime Minister Narendra Modi of BK's native India created a Ministry of Yoga, in order to promote India's ancient therapeutic traditions. For decades books had been written and talks given about the coming together of western science and Eastern spiritual practices for the greater good of both the East and West. There were gradual signs that this concept was sinking into American culture and having an impact, an impact on everything from physical health to mental health to emotional balance and self-control.

■ ■ ■

Our son was finding that out for himself. "When I went to a yoga class for the first time in my junior year in college," Eric told us, "I found that it was about compassion, not competition. At the beginning, the instructor told us that not everyone was going to look the same in the poses. We were told not to glance around the room during a pose and think, I'm not doing it right. That's how I have to look.

"The way you interact with the world every day doesn't apply in those classes. The fact that you're there and trying to participate is all that matters. When you start doing this, you step out of the paradigm that we're living inside of, where everyone is in competition with everyone else and we all have to do things the same way in school or at work or in society or wherever. It doesn't have to be that way all the time, and this thought process needs to be incorporated into people before they're twenty years old. Learn to take a conscious step away from what you've been doing and into something else. As an adult, you have to step away from the social influences and do something by *conscious intention*."

■ ■ ■

On December 14, 2012, two years to the day after the Sandy Hook shootings in Newtown, Connecticut, CBS's *60 Minutes* did a segment that alluded to this tragedy and Adam Lanza's mental illness. Later in the program, Anderson Cooper hosted another segment called "Mindfulness." Those interviewed for this feature talked about how cutting edge, high-tech companies were using the techniques of mindfulness to help their employees be less stressful and more productive. In the beginning, Cooper seemed very skeptical about how the simplicity of disconnecting oneself from the culture for a few minutes a day—and reconnecting to one's deeper, inner nature—could be beneficial. By the end of the show, he was talking about the transformative powers of these activities. He was talking about what an individual could do to lower his or her own level of anxiety and pressure—and by extension lower it in the society as a whole.

XXXII

In the fall of 2014, *Esquire* magazine published what may have been the first article ever attempting to penetrate the trauma and the humanity of a mass shooter—or in this case a potential shooter. It was a groundbreaking effort, for many reasons. No one outside of a handful of lawyers or mental health experts had yet been given a hint about what was inside James Holmes's spiral notebook or his medical or psychiatric records. Because of this, an emotional or psychological profile had never been publicly revealed about Holmes, due to the built-in conflict inside the American legal system. Yet a profile of someone who'd moved up to the edge of doing what Holmes had done was on full display in the *Esquire* story, which focused on an unnamed young man called "Trunk." With remarkable precision, his background fit into what we'd been hearing for more than two years about troubled young men with the capacity to evolve into mass shooters.

About a decade earlier, Trunk had been arrested in the middle of the night, while dressed all in black and armed with a .22-caliber pistol, a machete, a military-grade rifle slung across his back, and two thousand rounds of ammunition. He had two accomplices, who were similarly clad and armed. On the night they allegedly went out to unleash mayhem, they were stopped and arrested at three a.m. because of how late they were on the streets and of how they were dressed.

And then because the police quickly discovered that they were carrying an arsenal. Trunk eventually pled guilty to carjacking and was sentenced to ten years in prison.

Behind bars, he began to learn what he never had learned in the outside world: basic social skills, such as how to cope around other people, how to talk to them, and how to get along when your health or your life depended on it. Following his release from prison, he went to college, applied himself to his studies, and no longer had feelings about wanting to harm society.

For *Esquire*, he tried to articulate his long process of becoming a near-killer, which may have started when he was ten and his mother died or when he had to repeat seventh grade or when he began having a series of troubling thoughts: What was he doing wrong? Why didn't anyone like him? Why were his peers against him? How could he feel something different?

He could have told himself that he was a loser, he said to *Esquire*, but he didn't want to think of himself in that way. "So I started thinking *they* were losers," he said. "I started thinking that they didn't like me because they were afraid of me—because I had power and they didn't. Because I was special. And that's when it all really got started. When I began thinking I was special."

Like Holmes and other mass shooters, Trunk had kept a journal documenting his long tumble into darkness. Years after his arrest, he made a point of saying that he didn't want to become infamous by creating a massacre—the motive that many people have ascribed to the young killers. He wanted to be known and accepted for who he was *before* going through with it. He wanted to not feel the isolation that he imagined he was living in.

When he was a senior in high school some of his classmates had in fact reached out to him, but he was too shy or blinded by too much pain to see this or accept their friendship or help.

Eventually, he gravitated toward someone like himself—another young man who shared his feelings (à la Klebold and Harris)—and they played a lot of video games together, games about *"people who are special rising over everyone else to save the world."*

His father kept fourteen guns in the house (à la Adam Lanza)—military-grade weapons kept in a locked closet, plus lots of ammunition. Trunk acknowledged that if he'd had to go out in the world and buy his own firearms illegally, he'd had been too frightened to bring that off. But the guns were only a few feet away and became irresistible. Take someone with very low self-esteem, he said, and put a gun in his hands, and he feels "like a movie hero . . ."

What did he want more than anything else? To be able to relieve the stress and pressure building inside of him in some constructive way, rather than through mass violence. "I wanted *release*," he explained to *Esquire*. "It's not a desire for death. It's a desire for escape . . . Maybe if this happened, I'd feel calm. I'd feel the way *they* do. I'd feel peace."

The night before the planned attack, he lay in bed and thought to himself that someone had to do this, to make a statement and "shoulder the burden," so it might as well be him. At the same time, he admitted that if just one person had noticed how much torment he was in and had made the effort to come to him and say that he didn't have to do this and "you don't have to have this strange strength, we accept you," Trunk would have "broken down and given up."

The significant thing about Trunk, as with so many others like him who had gone on to become mass shooters, was that his emotional turmoil long preceded his desire for guns and his need to arm himself against a world that he perceived was hostile. He felt ineffectual and he wanted power, personal power, and to have an effect on the society he was living in and to make an impact that the larger culture could not ignore. He wanted to feel better and did not know how to do so.

Trunk essentially laid out for readers at least some of what the media and the general public, who paid for the legal system and were charged with participating in it through serving on juries, had thus far been prevented from learning about the Aurora shooter, more than two years after the massacre.

■ ■ ■

Following Holmes's second psychiatric exam, the judge set a new trial date of December 8, 2014. To the surprise of no one, the defense soon objected to this new development.

"I can guarantee the court we will not be prepared in that short of time frame . . ."public defender Tamara Brady told Judge Samour. "There is no way we will have all of this done."

Despite these protestations, the judge finally spoke up. "Yes, there's a lot of work to be done," he said. "But you have a lot of people, and you've had a lot of time."

On October 15, Dr. William Reid, the new psychiatric examiner who'd interviewed Holmes for twenty-two hours, handed in his report on time, and the case remained on schedule. A few days later, the defense asked for the trial to be delayed yet again. The prosecution agreed with this, and the trial date was now reset, for the fourth time, for January 20, 2015, exactly two and a half years, or thirty months, or more than nine hundred days, after the massacre. That was the date jury selection was to begin, with nine thousand people in Arapahoe County receiving summons to appear at the courthouse if called, and there were estimates that finding twelve people to sit in judgment of Holmes could take up to five months (some said even that was optimistic).

If the case did ever go to trial, the defense wanted the judge to instruct victims to control their emotions when testifying about the crime's impact on them. This was necessary to ensure that their testimony didn't "overwhelm the jurors with emotion," leading to an unfair sentence for Holmes.

The recommended defense instruction would say: "Your consideration of victim impact evidence must be limited to a rational inquiry into the culpability of Mr. Holmes, not an emotional response to the evidence. In rendering your sentencing verdict in this case, you must not be influenced by any sort of sympathy or sentiment for the victim's family."

In mid-November, with the trial only two months away, the defense asked Judge Samour to remove himself from the case. He quickly said no. In December, the defense asked for another delay in the start of the trial because of medical emergencies within their team. Again, the judge said no. "To delay this trial," he wrote in his order, "unnecessarily or improperly solely on the basis that this is a death penalty case would only promote the cynical view—sadly held by many—that the justice system is broken."

A month before jury selection was to begin, Holmes's parents, in their first-ever public statement, said that their son was not a monster, the trial should be called off, and he should be put in a mental institution for the rest of his life. Their remarks had no effect, and Melisa Cowden, whose ex-husband Gordon Cowden had been killed in the shooting, characterized the statement as comical.

■ ■ ■

As the legal proceedings ground on, politicians were focused on issues besides youthful violence. In the run-up to the 2014 midterm elections, those running for office in both parties talked about their fears over immigration and stopping the spread of Ebola in the United States, which had killed one American. As they campaigned, the Harvard School of Public Health, using a database created by *Mother Jones*, published findings showing that mass shootings in the country had tripled since 2011. They defined the shootings as attacks that "took place in public, in which the shooter and the victims generally were unrelated and unknown to each other, and in which the shooter murdered four or more people."

Former Arizona Congresswoman Gabrielle Giffords, who'd been seriously wounded in just such an attack that had killed six people, toured the country before the midterms, hoping to build support for more gun control. No one from either side of the aisle joined her. In October, as she was trying to call attention to mass violence, eighteen-year-old Matthew Ross, a student at Black Rock High School in Yucca Valley, California, was arrested for threatening to shoot and stab staff members because he didn't feel they were giving him enough respect. Inside Ross's home, the police found swords, crossbows, hatchets, hunting knives, firearms, and hundreds of rounds of rifle and shotgun ammunition.

Moms Demand Action started pressuring the Kroger supermarket chain to prohibit "open carry" after gun extremists used Kroger stores to demonstrate their "rights." Free speech, as many have reminded us over the years, is rarely free. Some gun activists got hold of personal photos of those supporting Moms Demand Action, Photoshopped them, and then posted them along with obscene comments.

■ ■ ■

That fall the FBI issued its own report and made official what everyone already knew: Mass shootings had become much more frequent in the past seven years. From 2000 through 2006, according to the feds' own study, there were 6.4 mass shooting incidences a year. From 2007 to 2013, there were 16.4 such events annually. In total, the mass shootings had killed 486 and wounded 557. Forty of the fifty states had seen mass shootings, as well as the District of Columbia, and no part of the country was immune from them. They occurred in small towns, big cities, and rural areas. The shooter usually acted alone, and of 160 such massacres, only six were done by women. Forty percent of the killers committed suicide at the scene, and 69 percent of the shootings were over in less than five minutes, before law enforcement could respond.

In 2014, board members in some Missouri school districts began sending faculty members to concealed-weapons training. That fall a 7,500-student Massachusetts school district, thirty miles north of Boston, implemented the country's first shooter-detection system, which could recognize and track a gunman roaming through the building. The "Guardian Indoor Gunshot Detection" technology was similar to that used by the military to keep soldiers safe across the globe. Sensors placed in the classrooms, entrances, and hallways detected the firing of a gunshot in less than a second. A mobile app sent a text message with the shooter's location to the superintendent, principal, police chief, and school resource officer. Officials could then track the gunman's movements, showing exactly where the assailant was in the building. High-tech military hardware was now on hand in the American school system.

■ ■ ■

Within the FBI's Critical Incident Response Group was the National Center for the Analysis of Violent Crime, and within it was Behavioral Analysis Unit 2, ten federal agents led by Andre Simons who were charged with assessing threats. BAU2 didn't create profiles of potential shooters as much as it asked for help from bystanders who noticed people showing signs of aberrant conduct—such as writing or saying incendiary things or nurturing a serious grudge. Has the person taken an interest in mass shooters or been warned away from an event? Or acquired firearms and spoken about a plan? Anyone with such information was asked to contact the FBI. Simons said that his office received three to four referrals about mass shootings each week. Their mission, Simons said, was to stop active-shooting incidents before they happened, and he called upon the public to help law enforcement do that. As awareness of the mass shootings rose, the FBI was starting to receive that assistance, when civilians noticed someone around them who was clearly troubled and talking about violence.

The little things, the small observations and actions that people took before the bloodshed exploded, mattered. In late 2013, U.S. Attorney General Eric Holder credited Simons and BAU2 with preventing 148 mass shootings and violent attacks. Since the creation of

BAU2 in 2010, the office has intervened in approximately five hundred potential mass shootings events that *didn't happen.*

"What these people need," Andre Simons told *Esquire,* "are alternatives to violence. They are often unable or unwilling to articulate to themselves that there are alternatives to violence. They have shut that door. Our job is to open other doors for them so that they don't go through the last door they think they have left."

■ ■ ■

The FBI's "Active Shooter Study" was itself a breakthrough: a national recognition of the depth and urgency of the mass-shooting problem. For the past two decades there had been little or no federal support for research into what some viewed as a major health issue— gun violence—that had left more than thirty thousand Americans dead every year. Congress had barred federal funds for gun violence research because they associated this with gun control. In 2013, President Obama directed the Centers for Disease Control and Prevention (CDC) and other federal labs to carry out this research and to put together prevention strategies.

The FBI study would help define the scope of the problem, so that states could better target their prevention programs. And for the first time ever, there was growing momentum around building a reliable national reporting database for firearm injuries and deaths. The CDC was offering more than $7 million in grants to states to expand its National Violent Death Reporting System. The hope was also to capture more data on firearm fatalities.

Right after the FBI made public its study, a curious thing happened in Jefferson County, which held the western suburbs of Denver. It also held Columbine High School. A group of students organized a series of walkouts from their classes, and by the fourth day of protest, one thousand students from Columbine, Dakota Ridge High, and Lakewood High were taking part in them. Beyond Colorado, hundreds of high schoolers from across the nation were also opposing a proposed curriculum calling for promoting "positive aspects" of U.S. history and avoiding or burying "civil disorder, social strife, or disregard of the law," of the kind carried out by Martin Luther King, Jr. The protests were largely orchestrated through Facebook.

As Savanna Barron, a senior at Lakewood High, told *The Denver Post* during one of the demonstrations, "People think because we are teenagers, we don't know things, but we are going home and looking things up. If they don't teach us civil disobedience, we will teach ourselves." The students' rallying slogan was: "It's our history, don't make it mystery."

■ ■ ■

In early October, California Governor Jerry Brown signed into law, mostly as a response to the Elliott Rodger massacre at Isla Vista, a bill allowing family members or police to seek a court order to temporarily remove lawfully owned weapons from the home of someone deemed at risk of committing violence. The "Gun Violence Restraining Order" bill arose after the horror of the Rodger rampage, in an effort to keep mentally unstable individuals from possessing firearms. While Rodger's parents had sought help from law enforcement before the shootings, he'd violated no law justifying police action. The new law would permit relatives to get a court order to confiscate weapons from a family member showing signs of violence. The bill lets police search a subject's residence and remove weapons. After mass shootings in their jurisdictions, Illinois, Virginia, and Connecticut put threat-assessment teams at all state-funded colleges. Change was taking place, as if the country was slowly awakening from a long sleep.

On the second anniversary of the Sandy Hook massacre, Everytown for Gun Safety, the nation's largest gun violence prevention organization, and Moms Demand Action for Gun Sense in America issued a report on the ninety-five school shootings since Adam Lanza's carnage in Newtown. The following day—December 15, 2014—the two groups held a press conference at the U.S. Capitol. They were joined by both of Connecticut's U.S. Senators, Democrats Richard Blumenthal and Chris Murphy; by U.S. Representative Mike Thompson, a California Democrat who chaired the U.S. House's Gun Violence Prevention Task Force; and by Pamela Wright of Chicago, whose seventeen-year-old son, Tyrone Lawson, was shot and killed in January 2013 following a high school basketball game. Senator Blumenthal spoke of the thousands of Americans killed by firearms since Sandy Hook and said that the best way to honor the memory of all of these victims was through action against gun violence. In mid-December, families of nine of the Sandy Hook victims also sued the makers and the sellers of the Bushmaster AR-15, used by Lanza in the shootings.

Interlude

For the past couple of years, Eric had worked at the Environmental Center at the University of Colorado in Boulder, and part of his job was picking up the trash on campus that people threw away, sometimes during football games, and then sorting out the recyclable material from the rest. More than once, he'd contrasted the difference between reading or talking about environmental issues in class and having his hands dirtied by wading through what others had discarded. Early in our discussions, he'd said that one learned how to be socialized and how to compromise by living with others and rubbing up against the differences between people on a daily basis. One also learned something about environmentalism by sifting through garbage.

Sometimes he'd complained about the work because it was demanding and tiring, but he'd liked its physical nature and seeing the results of his labor. He'd had a tangible effect, even if it was a small one, on a global problem. He'd *done* something instead of just complained about it. He'd served a cause greater than himself.

The small things, or supposedly small ones, kept coming up and refusing to stay small. Time and again in our discussions about the Holmes case, our son made the same comment: "Talk to your kids. Just talk to them and listen to what they have to say. You may not like it, but you need to listen to what they're thinking and experiencing. It all starts there. Everyone feels isolated now. Everyone feels that they don't really live in a community anymore."

One night at a dinner party, a very bright eighty-three-year-old woman asked us what book we were working on. We said the Holmes case, but with an emphasis on the cultural influences that had shaped him and his generation. After we spoke about this age group for a while, she asked, "Has your son ever felt needed?"

We told her about his work at the Environmental Center and about the late summer of 2013, when Boulder was hit by what meteorologists described as the kind of flood that might happen every eight hundred years. The house Eric was sharing with five other young men was inundated, the basement buried in water, and all of them spent days and nights scooping silt and water out of the house, salvaging whatever they could. The experience impacted Eric long after the water had receded; he'd felt needed in the middle of a deluge. A crisis wasn't just something to be victimized by, but an opportunity to discover more of your own strength, your own ability to make decisions and act, and your own inner resources. You were stronger and more resilient than you'd realized. The flood was not a large event in the grand scale of life on earth, but the more we probed the causes and effects behind the mass-shooting phenomenon, the more we returned to the smaller things, the small connections between human beings, or what we commonly refer to as small.

One of those things was a doorway with Eric that opened up in larger ways as he got older. It had started in middle school when we'd hear him singing Beatles songs, or tunes by Bob Marley, or Neil Young's "Old Man," or Led Zeppelin's "Ramble On." Like many parents of our generation, we were glad that the music of our era resonated with him. Then he began sharing the albums of contemporary artists like Green Day, Vampire Weekend, and others that had recorded material with both social and spiritual substance.

During his high school years, he'd continued our musical education, introducing us to hip hop and "sampling," which often used snippets of the music we'd grown up listening to. Since both of us were passionate about music and over the years had been involved in the making of it, we'd found more common ground with our son, and Joyce began adding some of his music to her digital library. While it was common ground, it wasn't always easy ground. Eric's favorite artists were rap and hip-hop stars, usually from ghettos in Brooklyn or elsewhere. He was particularly interested in the alternative hip-hop that revolved around issues of social justice in America, also called "Conscious Hip-Hop." This genre included New York artists like Yasiin Bey (formerly known as Mos Def), Talib Kweli, Common, A Tribe Called Quest, and others—but the first difficulty with these artists for his parents came in trying to understand their language.

They used phrases and inflections that could be hard to grasp, especially for those well into middle age. This was a challenge, but if we were willing to sit down and listen closely to what they were saying, or to read the lyrics Eric showed us online, we were surprised at what we found. The origins of hip-hop, like the origins of much of what we'd listened to in the 1960s, were rooted in social protest and the concepts of Afrocentricity and self-determination. There were striking similarities between the issues the Conscious Rappers were talking about (politics, racial and economic injustices) and what folk singers like Woody Guthrie, Pete Seeger, Bob Dylan, and others had done in the 1960s protest movements and before then. Only the form of the music was different now and the nuances of the English language. The convictions and the message were essentially the same: All of the artists were all interested in stopping abuses of power and spreading equality.

One afternoon when Eric was a senior in high school, the three of us were driving home from the mountains. He was in the back seat with headphones on, deep into his own music and thoughts. He looked up and asked if he could play a song through the car speaker. He put on the soundtrack of *Cadillac Records* with Mos Def performing a Chuck Berry song. It was the starting point for many more conversations about music and race.

Like Eric, Steve had grown up with a particular interest in black music: the blues of B. B. King, Muddy Waters, Howlin' Wolf, and Etta James, among many others. These artists didn't just introduce him to significant portions of African-American culture, but gave him a better understanding of black history and race relations in the United States. This was especially important for Steve, born in the 1950s in rural Kansas, when the civil rights movement was just beginning. Eric was now listening to a newer generation of black artists who were expanding his own consciousness on the subject of culture and race in America.

Music gave us insight into our son, into his peers whom he shared this music with, and into aspects of the current society that was producing these new artists. People his age had many of the same idealistic feelings we'd had when young—when our generation was striving for change and for making the United States "a more perfect union." By not dismissing Eric's music because it was challenging, we'd built another bridge.

The thing about America now, as opposed to when we were younger, was that you had to dig a little harder with everybody you met on the street or at a party or at work to find the shared dreams and desires. The sense of community was no longer as obvious, at least on the surface, but most people still had the same aspirations. And down below all of this was a deeper revelation: The government was no longer playing a parental role for us. It wasn't going to fix everything. Society was changing too fast, and was far too influenced by new technology, for any institution to keep up with it. Now, we had to find our own answers and build our own community through our own participation. The mass-shooting epidemic was just one piece of this much broader reality and much broader challenge. It was all a very loud and very misdirected call from young people for change.

EPILOGUE

Over the 2014 Thanksgiving holiday, Eric came home to visit—arriving just after a grand jury in Ferguson, Missouri, had refused to indict police officer Darren Wilson in the shooting death of an eighteen-year-old African-American man, Michael Brown. The lack of legal action against Wilson unleashed protests from coast to coast, the unrest bubbling up in the streets of America following what had been years, if not decades, of passivity and silence. The protests appeared to be about more than just this one event, and they seemed to represent something much larger and more cumulative—a sense of anger and frustration too long denied; a feeling that bullying of all kinds, either inside of schools or by police or by governments, was toxic and lethal; a sense that action and change were necessary, even if the latter hadn't yet taken shape. It all felt as if something organic was trying to rise up after being held down for so long.

A few days later, anger exploded again with the failure of a Staten Island grand jury to indict police officer Daniel Pantaleo in the choking death of another African-American man, Eric Garner. The streets of New York and other cities, reaching all the way to Berkeley, California, were now filled with pushback.

Sitting with Eric and watching the coverage of these protests brought us full circle from when we'd first begun talking with him about this book. The TV screen held precisely the kinds of images we'd come of age with in the 1960s and '70s, when the nation had seen numerous outbursts of social and political activism. Very unexpectedly, toward the end of 2014, a pulse was back in the air. People were starting to pay attention to uncomfortable issues that hadn't gone away just because they'd been ignored, but were becoming more prominent and more disruptive. Young and old, black and white, and many other races were marching together mile after mile through the streets of major American cities, stopping traffic and using civil disobedience as it had so often been used in the past to challenge injustice. Glimmers of something new were in the air, along with the feeling that all of us had a role to play in confronting these problems and finding solutions. We weren't merely observers of these events, but actors in them. Maybe there was something more to life than entertainment or extreme humor and cynicism— something more than ironic detachment and consuming the latest piece of technology.

The dulled-out, drugged-out, moral vacuum Americans had been living inside of for more than a decade was starting to crack. Instead of being told what our glossed-over history had been during those years, instead of being obedient to the dictates of what did not serve the common good, people were taking their own steps to make new history.

Following the killings in Missouri and Staten Island, Yasiin Bey said that this moment was "an opportunity for necessary change. Positive change. And it's not necessarily convenient or comfortable . . . I read somewhere that in order for an arrow to fly, the bow has to be drawn back. There's some pressure involved and I think we're all feeling that pressure. Some of us are more aware of it than others. Some of us are trying to drown it out. But we all feel it one way or another in indelible ways in these times and days."

■ ■ ■

With forty other reporters, we sat in the courtroom on Tuesday, January 20, 2015, the first day of jury selection and exactly thirty months after the shootings. The seasons had rolled over yet again, and a dusting of snow set on the trees east of Denver, sunlight illuminating the frost on this cold winter morning. At the courthouse, snipers patrolled the roofs as they had at the initial legal proceedings in the torrid summer of 2012, and nationwide media were again on hand for the beginnings of the trial. Of the nine thousand jury summonses originally sent out across Arapahoe County, two thousand had fallen by the wayside because these people no longer resided in the jurisdiction. A few hundred of the remaining seven thousand—the first batch of prospective jurors—were in court today filling out an eighteen-page questionnaire for the judge, the lawyers, and the defendant. Surrounded by his legal team, Holmes was dressed in civilian clothing, wearing a blue sport coat, striped button-down shirt, and khakis. He had on dark-rimmed glasses, looking less like a criminal now and more like the young scholar he was when relocating to Aurora in 2011. He seemed alert and thoughtful but had no visible involvement in the jury selection process. His trousers concealed a cable that ran down the inside of his pant leg and bolted him to the floor.

As Judge Samour informed the attorneys and media (there were virtually no spectators on hand) about the long and demanding ordeal in front of them, he made a point of asking everyone to be civil in court and not to waste his time with frivolous arguments. While his words were an appropriate plea to keep things moving forward, the entire event seemed peculiarly hollow and empty, given how long the living victims and the aggrieved families of the dead had waited for the trial to begin. So far the case had seen 1,700 motions, hearings, and orders, while costing the public $5.5 million. Two and a half years had gone by without anyone outside the legal system learning anything of significance about Holmes or his state of mind at the time of the massacre. For thirty months, no one beyond a tiny handful of people knew what was inside the spiral notebook or what it revealed about the mental health of Holmes at the time of crime—the only relevant factor in this case. More months would pass before any psychiatric testimony would make its way into the courtroom, and it was possible that the notebook's contents would never be revealed. One wondered if, like the notorious basement tapes made by Columbine killers Eric Harris and Dylan Klebold, which were destroyed by the Jefferson County (Colorado) Sheriff's Department in 2011, it ultimately would be suppressed.

The only significant question was *why* Holmes had done what he'd done and if he was sane or not on July 20, 2012. Far too many obstacles had stood between the time of the shootings and this Tuesday morning in January 2015. In this particular set of circumstances, due process and the endless maneuvering of lawyers felt deeply inadequate because we'd been cut off from the information that could be most useful. To date there was nothing in the legal system's response to the massacre that had held any meaning for those observing it. The system felt broken or badly crippled—and that had sucked all the air out of the case and out of the courtroom by the start of jury selection.

We live in a profoundly violent society, and we want to know more about what's driving this phenomenon and the young people who are pulling the triggers. We want to know what is possible to know when a shooter survives, but by January 2015 everything surrounding James Holmes felt deflated and depressed. That might well change as his trial unfolds, but at the moment, one had to look elsewhere for passion and meaning around this tragedy.

Five days before the start of jury selection, a sixteen-year-old suburban Denver high school junior, Abby Javernick, wrote an editorial in *The Denver Post*. She reminded readers that in her lifetime there had been six major school shootings or incidents in Colorado, and she called this "inexcusable." After mentioning Columbine, she wrote, "Here we are, fifteen years later, and the only difference . . . is that now students are constantly on their guard, knowing escape routes and hiding places, police at the ready . . ."

She called upon gun owners to take safety classes, register their weapons, and submit to mental health examinations. She pointed out how she and her classmates had spent hours rehearsing what to do if an active shooter entered her school: "Where's the closest exit? If I can't get out in time, where will I go? If the shooter finds me, what will I do? If I have the ability to stop the shooter, how will I disarm him? . . . I'm sick of going to school, hearing the intercom click on, and praying that it's just another announcement. . . . So I plead—no, I *demand*—a change. I should be able to go to school without fearing for my life, and I hardly think that's too much to ask."

■ ■ ■

Small things, small steps, small pieces of writing, small voices, and small change all mattered. Seemingly minor steps could help people to overcome inertia, to stop feeling helpless, to join with others, and to find their own strength and hope. Once they felt hope, anything was possible. But there always had to be a starting point, an opening up of a new discussion, an end to the feeling of resignation in the face of being victimized by outside forces. The mass-shooting phenomenon wasn't "out there" in some other state or some other city or some other family, but much closer and more intimate than that. We are all vulnerable to it, all involved in it, and all capable of altering the environment in which we live.

Our journey toward understanding more about this violence had started at home, with a handful of words from our son, and those words had carried us across the country to speak with others who wanted to do something to stop the horror and to make the victims' lives count for something. We all wanted the same thing, and what we'd learned was stunningly simple: Get involved. Be a participant. Take a chance. Speak up—like Abby. See this as an opportunity, a moment to connect with others and to create something new. Ask a question, ask a follow-up question, and then listen carefully. Don't be satisfied with surfaces. Don't think that you don't matter. Keep asking questions and keep listening, and there's no telling what you might hear or where those words might lead you or what you might do next.

A different kind of social interaction and community, Kira Jones had said after living in Spain, is what's missing from our culture. Everyone has a role to play in reclaiming our common humanity.

Dare to imagine that you *can* have an effect. You could be the one who makes the difference.

ACKNOWLEDGMENTS

We couldn't have written this particular book without the help and insights of our son, Eric. During many road trips throughout the West and living room discussions, he spoke honestly about himself and the people his age. In nonfiction books, you always need at least one person to guide you into the subject matter and who's willing to give you the time you need. Eric did that and pointed us in the direction that allowed us to think about the mass-shooting phenomenon in a broader and more social context. His voice became the first one of his generation to assist us. We thank him and all the other millennials who later agreed to share their perspectives. We also deeply appreciate those in the medical/psychiatric fields and the other professionals who took the time to share their knowledge and experience with us.

We're grateful for the book's editor, Dan Smetanka, who did a tremendous job of helping us shape and refine the narrative. He understood what we were trying to do in *The Spiral Notebook*, and his encouragement and enthusiasm inspired us. His deft touch with a manuscript is everywhere in these pages, as is his critical thinking and his ability to see the larger subject in this story. Finally, our agent, Mel Berger of William Morris Endeavor, put us together with Dan and Counterpoint Press. It's been a very rewarding collaboration.